The
Unknown
Sayings of
Jesus

Marvin Meyer

New Seeds
Boston & London
2005

New Seeds Books
An imprint of
Shambhala Publications, Inc.
Horticultural Hall
300 Massachusetts Avenue
Boston, Massachusetts 02115
www.shambhala.com

9 8 7 6 5 4 3 2 1

First New Seeds Edition
Printed in the United States of America

♾ This edition is printed on acid-free paper
that meets the American National Standards
Institute z39.48 Standard.

Distributed in the United States
by Random House, Inc., and in Canada by
Random House of Canada Ltd

Designed by Graciela Galup

Library of Congress Cataloging-in-Publication Data
The unknown sayings of Jesus/[edited by] Marvin Meyer.
p. cm.
Translated into English from Coptic, Syriac, and other languages.
Originally published: 1st ed. San Francisco: HarperSanFrancisco, c. 1998.
Includes bibliographical references (p.   ).
ISBN 1-59030-274-5 (pbk.: alk. paper)
1. Jesus Christ—Words—Extra-canonical parallels. I. Meyer, Marvin W.
BS2970.U55 2005
232.9′54—dc22   2005014377

Contents

Acknowledgments

vii

Introduction

ix

THE UNKNOWN SAYINGS OF JESUS

1

Notes

147

Selected Bibliography

173

What kind of a living person is Jesus? Don't search for formulas to describe him, even if they be hallowed by centuries. I almost got angry the other day when a religious person said to me that only someone who believes in the resurrection of the body and in the glorified body of the risen Christ can believe in the living Jesus. . . . Let me explain it in my way. The glorified body of Jesus is to be found in his sayings.

—ALBERT SCHWEITZER, from a sermon he preached at St. Nicolai's Church on Sunday, November 19, 1905 (*Reverence for Life*, p. 65)

Acknowledgments

I WOULD LIKE to acknowledge the help of several people and organizations who have facilitated the production of this book. The Griset Chair in Religion and the Wang-Fradkin Professorship at Chapman University, as well as the J. W. and Ida M. Jameson Foundation and the Board of Higher Education of the United Methodist Church, have provided generous support for this project. Gesine Schenke Robinson has made available to me the unpublished Coptic text of Berlin 20915, with permission to translate and publish a saying in the text, and Charles W. Hedrick and Paul A. Mirecki, along with Polebridge Press, have allowed me to have access to the Coptic text and English translation of Berlin 22220 prior to publication. Ra'id Faraj of Chapman University has assisted me by checking the Arabic of Islamic sayings of Jesus. Among the other colleagues who have assisted me and have offered useful advice, I mention in particular Jon Ma. Asgeirsson and Saw Lah Shein of the Institute for Antiquity and Christianity, Claremont Graduate

University. Several people at Harper San Francisco have given significant help, most notably my editor, John Loudon, who urged me to undertake this project and watched over the preparation of the book. At Shambhala Publications, Dave O'Neal guided the book into its new life with a new press. Finally, I thank my wife and children for their years of patience with me as I have poked around curious corners of late antiquity in search of unknown sayings of Jesus.

Marvin Meyer
Chapman University

Introduction

BEYOND THE NEW TESTAMENT gospels, beyond Q, and beyond the Gospel of Thomas lies another set of sources for our knowledge of Jesus of Nazareth, a set of sources I call the unknown sayings of Jesus.

The New Testament gospels, especially the synoptic Gospels of Matthew, Mark, and Luke, with their narrative accounts of the acts of Jesus and their rehearsal of his sayings, are valuable sources for our study both of who Jesus was and of how he has been interpreted. For instance, the New Testament gospel authors provide significant glimpses into what Jesus did in first-century Palestine, but they also interpret, modify, and design acts of Jesus as they proclaim him to early hearers and readers. Similarly, the New Testament gospel authors echo the sayings that Jesus spoke in first-century Palestine, but they also edit, rephrase, and create sayings of Jesus as they apply the teachings of the living Jesus—for he was believed to continue to live and speak in the Christian communities—to the needs of early hearers and readers.

Q and the Gospel of Thomas, with their portrayals of Jesus as a teacher of wisdom whose legacy consists of his sagacious sayings placed one after another in a long series of insightful utterances, are also valuable sources particularly for our study of sayings of Jesus. Both Q and the Gospel of Thomas, I propose, contain sayings materials that antedate the New Testament gospels; thus, these sayings may not only be closer to what Jesus actually said but may also highlight the editorial modifications incorporated into the New Testament gospels. For example, the parables of Jesus in the Gospel of Thomas are presented simply as stories, as Jesus presumably told them, without the allegorical amplifications that explain the parables and control their interpretation in the synoptic gospels.

Q (from German *Quelle,* "source," for "sayings source") is the sayings collection that no longer exists as a separate document but may be reformulated through a careful comparison of Matthew, Mark, and Luke. Most scholars now concur that Q was once a written sayings collection used independently by Matthew and Luke (who also used an edition of Mark) as they wrote their gospels. Because of Q, the strong, relatively silent Jesus of Mark becomes the garrulous Jesus of Matthew and Luke, preaching the sermon on the mount and four other long sermons in Matthew and engaging in a ser-

mon on the plain and ongoing conversation on the road
in Luke.

The Gospel of Thomas is the sayings gospel that was
discovered near Nag Hammadi, Egypt, in 1945 and that
now may be linked to the Papyrus Oxyrhynchus fragments 1, 654, and 655 (see Unknown Sayings 1–21, from
what we may now call the Greek Gospel of Thomas). It
is increasingly apparent to many of us that the Gospel of
Thomas should be taken seriously as an early and independent source of sayings of Jesus, with some materials
that go back, like Q, to the first century. (Compare, for
instance, Gospel of Thomas saying 17 and the Dialogue
of the Savior 56–57, cited here in Unknown Saying 71,
with 1 Corinthians 2:9, where Paul seems to cite the
saying as a wisdom saying of Jesus.) Yet it is also clear
that both the Gospel of Thomas and Q, like the New
Testament gospels, edit the sayings of Jesus to meet the
needs of their own communities. (For translations and
discussions of Q and the Gospel of Thomas, see John S.
Kloppenborg, *Q Parallels: Synopsis, Critical Notes, and
Concordance*; John S. Kloppenborg, Marvin W. Meyer,
Stephen J. Patterson, and Michael G. Steinhauser, *Q—
Thomas Reader*; Burton L. Mack, *The Lost Gospel: The Book
of Q and Christian Origins*; Marvin Meyer, *The Gospel of
Thomas: The Hidden Sayings of Jesus*; Robert J. Miller, edi-
tor, *The Complete Gospels: Annotated Scholars Version;* and

James M. Robinson, Paul Hoffmann, and John S. Kloppenborg, editors, *The Critical Edition of Q*

The unknown sayings of Jesus published here consist of sayings of Jesus recorded in sources—Christian, Jewish, and Muslim—other than the New Testament, Q, and the Gospel of Thomas. Throughout early Christian literature there are statements about people remembering the sayings of Jesus—whether in a more historically accurate or a more creative way. For instance, Acts 20:35 refers to followers of Jesus "remembering the sayings of the master Jesus, for he himself said, 'It is more blessed to give than to receive.'" In the Secret Book of James, from which several unknown sayings of Jesus are taken here (Unknown Sayings 90–113), the following compositional scenario is presented: "Now the twelve followers [were] all sitting together, recalling what the savior had said to each of them, whether in a hidden or an open manner, and organizing it in books. [And I] was writing what is in my [book]" (2,7–16). The Church History of Eusebius of Caesarea quotes Papias, a second-century church leader, describing how Matthew compiled an early Aramaic collection of sayings of Jesus under the title "Interpretation of the Sayings of the Master," a collection that may remind us a bit of Q. Such statements about remembering, recalling, and compiling sayings of Jesus show that other folks, apart from the authors of the New

Testament gospels, Q, and the Gospel of Thomas, were also busy working on sayings of Jesus. These other folks and their sayings of Jesus occupy our attention here.

Serious scholarly research on unknown sayings of Jesus, at times dubbed *agrapha*, or "unwritten" sayings of Jesus, has been going on for about a century. These sayings have sometimes been called "unwritten sayings" by scholars who have theorized that they go back to a group of Jesus' sayings that were transmitted orally and that constitute another authoritative source besides the New Testament. Near the end of the nineteenth century Alfred Resch published his work, *Agrapha: Aussercanonische Schriftfragmente*, in which he collected a large number of extracanonical sayings of Jesus and argued that some of them derive from a very early sayings gospel that included sayings of the historical Jesus. Resch maintained that this was a sayings source, reminiscent of the source described by Papias, that played a major role as an original gospel shaping the New Testament tradition.

Although Resch's basic thesis has proved to be controversial and has not convinced most scholars, his interest in the *agrapha*, or extracanonical sayings of Jesus, has carried the day, and other scholars have continued collecting and examining these sayings. Recently William D. Stroker published an extensive collection of these sayings under the title *Extracanonical Sayings of*

Jesus. Stroker organizes the sayings according to the form-critical categories developed by Rudolf Bultmann in *History of the Synoptic Tradition*, and while his is in many respects an excellent collection, it is flawed, in my estimation, by the exclusion of many sayings from the Nag Hammadi library and Islamic literature. Now another collection of these sayings has just appeared, assembled by William G. Morrice and entitled *Hidden Sayings of Jesus: Words Attributed to Jesus Outside the Four Gospels.* This is also a useful collection, and it includes what Morrice calls "Arabic gems," but an unfortunate canonical shadow seems to fall over the collection. At the end of his work Morrice observes that "it is surprising how little of value survives outside the New Testament" (p. 201). My own conclusion differs greatly from Morrice's. (For further discussion of and scholarly research on the *agrapha*, along with bibliography, see Resch, *Agrapha*, pp. 1–22; James Hardy Ropes, "Agrapha"; Joachim Jeremias, *Unknown Sayings of Jesus* [2nd ed.], pp. 1–43; Stroker, *Extracanonical Sayings of Jesus*, pp. 1–7; and Morrice, *Hidden Sayings of Jesus,* pp. 201–16.)

This book, *The Unknown Sayings of Jesus*, provides a sizable collection of sayings of Jesus not to be found in the New Testament, Q, or the Gospel of Thomas. Two hundred sayings are presented here in English translation;

that number is quite arbitrary, though two hundred sayings do make this collection roughly the size of Q. Of the hundreds of sayings that could be included in such a collection, I have selected a sample that is large enough to illustrate the variety found in the tradition of unknown sayings of Jesus. (I have also managed to sneak a few extra unknown sayings into the notes.) For the serious student whose appetite is not satisfied by the size of this collection, the bibliography opens up possibilities for additional reading.

These sayings are designated as "unknown" for three reasons. First of all, this designation places the present collection in line with earlier studies of these sayings by using the same terminology that Jeremias used. Second, this designation reflects the actual situation in the study of Jesus and his sayings. To many people, including many scholars, these sorts of sayings are relatively unknown, and they have often been neglected in the study of traditions relating to Jesus. Third, this designation recalls the traditional way of describing noncanonical sayings and sources as apocryphal, or "hidden," and accentuates the fact that they have been kept from the eyes of the faithful within Christianity. Now, at last, what was hidden can be disclosed, and unknown sayings of Jesus can be brought to light.

The arrangement of the two hundred sayings in this collection is also somewhat arbitrary. This is not a vice in a collection of Jesus' sayings, since we detect more than a little of this sort of arbitrary arrangement in sayings sources like the Gospel of Thomas. (The differences in order and arrangement observed by comparing the Coptic and Greek editions of the Gospel of Thomas are instructive in this regard.) There is, however, a modest organizational thread running through this collection. For the most part, sayings are clustered together here according to source, and the source for each saying is indicated in parentheses after the translation of the saying itself. The source that opens the collection is the Greek Gospel of Thomas, which is included here because the Oxyrhynchus papyrus fragments represent Greek editions of the Gospel of Thomas that differ from the Coptic version from the Nag Hammadi library. Following these sayings are two testimonies apparently giving variant readings from still other versions of the Gospel of Thomas (Sayings 22–23), and these are followed by sayings from Jewish-Christian gospels (Sayings 24–38) and the Gospel of the Egyptians (Sayings 39–43), both of which may be related to the Gospel of Thomas. Without a doubt some of the sayings of the Book of Thomas (Sayings 44–56) are related to the Gospel of Thomas, as are sayings from the Dialogue of the Savior (Sayings 57–77), and perhaps also the Gospel of Mary (Sayings 78–81). Since the sayings in the Gospel of Philip (Sayings 82–89) and the Secret Book of James (Sayings 90–113) derive, like the Gospel of Thomas and some of the sources that occur near the opening of this collection, from the Nag Hammadi library, they come next. Then, in rough chronological order, with thematic connections, come the sayings that give alternate readings in New Testament gospel manuscripts (Sayings 114–17); sayings that come from the so-called apostolic fathers, papyrus gospel fragments, and apocryphal acts of the apostles (Sayings 118–31); and sayings that are to be found in a wide variety of early Christian sources (Sayings 132–80). The collection concludes with sayings that are to be found in Jewish (Sayings 181–82) and Islamic sources (Sayings 183–200).

I consider the inclusion of sayings of Jesus from Jewish and Islamic sources to be indispensable for this collection. (Except for a brief reference in the note to Unknown Saying 119, the Jewish life of Jesus entitled *Toledot Yeshu* lies beyond the scope of this book; see the books by Joseph Klausner and Günter Schlichting listed in the bibliography.) Stroker seems to deemphasize the sayings of Jesus from Jewish sources and decided not to include sayings of Jesus from Islamic sources in his collection. He asserts that the sayings from Islamic sources are too numerous and too late to be listed in his *Extracanonical Sayings of Jesus*. Ropes includes two sayings from the Jewish

Talmud (see Unknown Sayings 181–82) as well as fifty-one sayings from Islamic sources, but he comments, "The Agrapha from Mohammedan sources are chiefly of merely curious interest" ("Agrapha," p. 344). I disagree with both Stroker's decision and Ropes's evaluation. The historical Jesus was a Jewish teacher, and the figure of Jesus is revered as a Muslim prophet. Admittedly, Jewish assessments of Jesus are frequently polemical, since they are caught up in the debates and disagreements that have often raged between Jewish and Christian people, and it is also true that Islamic sayings of Jesus are found in large numbers (Michael Asin y Palacios collected 233 of them) in rather late sources. Yet I believe the sayings of Jesus in Jewish and Islamic sources merit as serious a reading and consideration as the sayings in Christian sources; I suspect some may finally be judged to be sayings reflecting what the historical Jesus once said. After all, the sayings of Jesus in Islamic sources are presented within a tradition free of the christological burden of developing interpretations of Jesus that could proclaim him the Christian savior. I appreciate Jeremias's somewhat more balanced assessment of the sayings of Jesus in Islamic sources; for example, Jeremias includes Unknown Saying 200, "This world is a bridge," in an appendix in his book, and he is willing to consider the possibility that it originated in a primitive tradition.

The primary purpose of this book is to present a collection of unknown sayings of Jesus in English translation. Most of the English translations are my own. In a few instances I have produced translations that are adapted from other English translations, and whenever possible, in these instances, I have consulted additional translations as well as texts in ancient languages. Thus, the translations of Saying 37, preserved in Syriac, and Sayings 132–33, preserved in Ethiopic, are adapted from Wilhelm Schneemelcher, editor, *New Testament Apocrypha*, 1.162, 262, 268; the translation of Saying 134, preserved in Slavonic, is adapted from R. P. Casey and R. W. Thomson, "A Dialogue Between Christ and the Devil," p. 57; the translation of Saying 170, preserved in Syriac, is adapted from Jacob Neusner, *Aphrahat and Judaism*, p. 67; the translations of Sayings 181–82 are adapted from Isidore Epstein, editor, *The Babylonian Talmud*, 8.571, 29.84–85, R. Travers Herford, *Christianity in Talmud and Midrash*, pp. 138–39, 146–47, and Ropes, "Agrapha," p. 348; the translations of Sayings 183–84 are adapted from Shlomo Pines, *The Jewish Christians of the Early Centuries of Christianity According to a New Source*, p. 13, and S. M. Stern, "'Abd al-Jabbār's Account," p. 133; the translations of Sayings 185–200 are adapted from D. S. Margoliouth, "Christ in Islam," passim, James Robson, *Christ in Islam*, passim, Jeremias, *Unknown Sayings of Jesus*, p. 112, and the Latin translations in Michael Asin, *Logia et Agrapha Domini Jesu*, passim. The unpublished Coptic text of Saying 151 has been made available to me by Gesine Schenke Robinson, and is used with her permission. Unknown Saying 83 may be considered to have been uttered by Philip, but I have included it here because it illustrates some of the ambiguity involved in determining the attribution of sayings. Saying 199 is technically not a saying at all, but I have included it because of its value as an indication of nonverbal communication and because it demonstrates the application of a Cynic *chreia*, or useful statement, to Jesus (see the relevant note). For each unknown saying, a note appears at the back of the book suggesting a few parallels from other sources.

In the translations I employ the following signs:

[ ] Square brackets indicate a lacuna or gap in the text.

< > Pointed brackets indicate a correction of a scribal omission or error.

( ) Parentheses indicate material that is not present in the text but is supplied by the translator for the sake of clarity in the translation.

. . . Three dots within square brackets indicate that a word or words cannot be restored

with confidence. Three dots by themselves indicate an ellipsis—that is, the omission of a sec-
tion of the text from the translation.

↓ The occasional use of arrows indicates the
horizontal or vertical direction of fibers on papyrus pages.

The use of these signs will help the reader imagine some
of the problems and challenges encountered in translat-
ing and understanding the original texts.

It could be argued that the greatest significance of the unknown sayings of Jesus lies in their contribution to our
understanding of the transmission and development of
sayings of Jesus. Both within and outside the New Testament we can observe something of the complex process
through which sayings of Jesus were remembered—
initially, it seems, as part of oral lore—and applied to the
needs of communities of believers. Sometimes sayings of
Jesus were remembered more or less as he had spoken
them, but more often they were modified, and at times
new sayings of Jesus were created. On occasion, sayings
from other sources altogether were placed on the lips
of Jesus, perhaps like Gospel of Thomas saying 102
(cited here at Unknown Saying 188), which closely re-
sembles one of Aesop's fables, known also from Lucian

of Samosata. (Compare my notes in this book and in *The Gospel of Thomas* for this example and others.) All these sayings of Jesus could be passed on as individual sayings; organized into collections like Q, the Gospel of Thomas, and other sayings collections; or contextualized in narrative gospels like those in the New Testament and other texts. Our knowledge of this fascinating process is advanced considerably through a careful study of the unknown sayings presented here.

Doubtless some of these unknown sayings reflect what the historical Jesus actually said, and this prospect is exciting indeed. What new sayings and teachings of Jesus of Nazareth might we discover among the sources of unknown sayings? We must admit, however, that few if any of the sayings of Jesus preserved in written sources are likely to reproduce exactly what Jesus did say. After all, Jesus spoke Aramaic as his native language, though he may well have been able to speak some Greek. (And in his book *Honest to Jesus: Jesus for a New Millennium*, Robert W. Funk maintains that Jesus also spoke *basileia*, or "kingdom-talk," a form of speech communicating his vision of God's kingdom or reign among people.) Furthermore, in the documented sayings of Jesus, his oral speech is transformed into the written word, and this transformation from the spoken to the written word is a profound one. For example, presumably the parables of Jesus recounted in many sources, including the unknown sayings of Jesus, are compact written synopses of what Jesus the storyteller said in a more expansive way.

Nonetheless, Jesus' unknown sayings may still prove useful for our study of the sayings and teachings of Jesus of Nazareth if we are able to identify, within the large and diverse collection, sayings and motifs that reflect the historical Jesus and not the editorializing of later authors. This task of identifying sayings of the historical Jesus has proved to be a daunting one, not to be undertaken by those faint of heart or weak in resolve.

I can only sketch here three sets of criteria that may be used as guidelines for those who wish to try to identify which unknown sayings may be sayings of the historical Jesus. While these sets of criteria have not been universally accepted by scholars and should not be used uncritically, they may suggest a reasonable methodology that we can use in sorting through the sayings materials. We will look briefly here at the traditional formal criteria of Dennis C. Duling and Norman Perrin, the triadic formal criteria of John Dominic Crossan, and the more material criteria of Robert W. Funk.

In their book *The New Testament* (pp. 520–23), Duling and Perrin list four criteria that may help to determine whether a given saying reflects the historical Jesus. These criteria are formal standards that have been discussed by scholars for some time, and they may help describe how a saying of Jesus relates to other sayings, themes, and cultural features of Jesus' world. The first criterion is both the most important and the most controversial, for a rigorous application of this criterion may yield too radical an image of Jesus—an image of a Jesus who is completely out of sync with his own Jewish environment and the emerging Christian environment. These four criteria are the following:

1. Distinctiveness, or dissimilarity: Does the saying in question stand in some contrast to the conventional values of Judaism and Christianity, which have, after all, contributed so much to the development and interpretation of sayings of Jesus?
2. Multiple attestation: Does the saying reflect themes that are common and widespread in traditions about Jesus?
3. Coherence: Is the saying consistent with other sayings that are considered historically accurate?
4. Linguistic and environmental tests: Does the saying reflect the language and the cultural environment of first-century Palestine?

In his study *The Historical Jesus: The Life of a Mediter-ranean Jewish Peasant* (pp. xxvii–xxxiv), Crossan describes his rather complex methodology by focusing on triads; his second triad addresses textual problems. Seeking some sort of formal objectivity, Crossan develops three steps that may lead to a clarification of what the histori-cal Jesus may have said. The three steps are these:

1. Inventory: Declare and describe all the sources and texts to be used for the study of the historical Jesus.
2. Stratification: Position all the sources and texts in a chronological sequence. (Crossan isolates four strata — 30–60, 60–80, 80–120, 120–150 C.E.)
3. Attestation: Evaluate the sayings and themes from the stratified sources and texts used in the study of the historical Jesus according to multi-plicity of independent attestation.

Crossan's emphasis on multiplicity of independent attestation seems to build on Duling and Perrin's crite-rion of multiple attestation, but Crossan's formulation is more sophisticated. Crossan admits that the first and oldest stratum is in general the most significant — though subsequent strata may also reproduce early tra-ditions about Jesus — and he posits that "at least for the first stratum, everything is original until it is argued otherwise" (p. xxxii). (Contrast this stance with Duling and Perrin's criterion of distinctiveness.) Thus, Crossan concludes, "Plural attestation in the first stratum (that is, in the earliest texts) pushes the trajectory back as far as it can go with at least formal objectivity" (p. xxxiii).

In his article "Criteria for Determining the Authentic Sayings of Jesus" (pp. 8–10), Funk takes a different approach. He suggests five "locators" that can help to describe, in a more material way, basic features of the sayings and teachings of Jesus. These locators are more descriptive of the contents and styles of the sayings of Jesus than the other criteria (though the third locator may be compared in some ways to the criterion of distinctiveness). Funk's five locators are as follows:

1. Jesus said things that were short, pithy, and memorable.
2. Jesus spoke in aphorisms (short, pithy, memorable sayings) and in parables (short, short stories about some unspecified subject matter).
3. Jesus' language was distinctive.
4. Jesus' sayings and parables have an edge.
5. Jesus' sayings and parables characteristically call for a reversal of roles or frustrate ordinary, everyday expectations: they surprise and shock.

For further discussion of these criteria and what Funk now calls the "voice print" of Jesus, see *Honest to Jesus*, especially chapter 8, "The Search for the Rhetorical Jesus."

In the unknown sayings of Jesus published here, Jesus speaks in a richly diverse manner. He appears as a Jewish teacher of wisdom who advocates poverty, homelessness, and simplicity of life, calling on people to observe a vegetarian diet and to "fast from the world," yet he affirms that no one is richer than he. Jesus identifies with children, whores, and tax collectors; he criticizes the power brokers of his day; and he is chagrined by the behavior of the truly unclean people around him. He discusses his immediate family and addresses the members of that family, but he envisions a new order of family and sees other people as playing the roles of his mother and brothers and sisters. He respects his "mother the spirit," but he criticizes the "works of the female." He encourages people to come to know themselves, to discover themselves and the divine as well as the presence of Jesus within, while he maligns them for their childish ways and imperfect accomplishments. He discusses everyday features of life—lilies of the field, a date palm shoot and a head of grain, wine and thorns, latrines, graves, and dead dogs—but he resorts to statements of reversal and metaphor and parable as he proclaims God and God's kingdom. Many of his sayings are (as Funk puts it) short and pithy, but many others are fleshed out into discourses, questions and answers, and dialogues. Many of his sayings are enigmatic, and Jesus comments on these obscure sayings by announcing, "[Whoever finds the interpretation] of these sayings will not taste [death]" (Greek Gospel of Thomas saying 1, Unknown Saying 2).

Finally, we note that Jesus' well-known summons to seek and find is repeated several times in several ways throughout these sayings. May this summons function as an invitation to the reader to probe these unknown sayings and strive to hear the voice of Jesus still present in these words.

THE UNKNOWN SAYINGS OF JESUS

The hidden sayings of the living Jesus

These are the [hidden] sayings [that] the living Jesus spoke [and Judas, who is] also (called) Thomas, [recorded]. *(Greek Gospel of Thomas prologue, in Papyrus Oxyrhynchus 654.1–3)*

Whoever finds the interpretation of these sayings

And he said, "[Whoever finds the interpretation] of these sayings will not taste [death]." *(Greek Gospel of Thomas saying 1, in Papyrus Oxyrhynchus 654.3–5)*

LET ONE WHO SEEKS NOT STOP

[Jesus says], "Let one who [seeks] not stop [seeking until] one finds. When one finds, [one will be astonished, and having been] astonished, one will reign, and [having reigned], one will [rest]." *(Greek Gospel of Thomas saying 2, in Papyrus Oxyrhynchus 654.5–9)*

GOD'S KINGDOM IS INSIDE AND OUTSIDE

Jesus says, "[If] your leaders [say to you, 'Look], the kingdom is in heaven,' the birds of heaven [will precede you. If they say] that it is under the earth, the fish of the sea [will enter, and will precede] you. And [God's kingdom] is inside you [and outside (you). Whoever] knows [oneself] will find this. [And when you] know yourselves, [you will understand that] you are [children] of the [living] father. [But if] you do [not] know yourselves, [you are] in [poverty], and you are the [poverty]." *(Greek Gospel of Thomas saying 3, in Papyrus Oxyrhynchus 654.9–21)*

The First Will Be Last

[Jesus says], "A [person old in] days will not hesitate to ask a [little child seven] days old about the place of [life, and] that person will [live]. For many of the [first] will be [last, and] the last first, and they [will become one.]" *(Greek Gospel of Thomas saying 4, in Papyrus Oxyrhynchus 654.21–27)*

Know what is before your face

Jesus says, "[Know what is before] your face, and [what is hidden] from you will be disclosed [to you. For there is nothing] hidden that [will] not [become] revealed, and (nothing) buried that [will not be raised]." *(Greek Gospel of Thomas saying 5, in Papyrus Oxyrhynchus 654.27–31)*

Do not lie or do what you hate

[His followers] ask him [and] say, "How [shall we] fast? [How shall] we [pray]? How [shall we give to charity]? What [diet] shall [we] observe?"

Jesus says, "[Do not lie, and] do not do [what] you [hate, because all things are apparent before] truth. [For there is nothing] hidden [that will not be revealed]." *(Greek Gospel of Thomas saying 6, in Papyrus Oxyrhynchus 654.32–40)*

Compare also Gospel of Thomas saying 14: "Jesus said to them, 'If you fast, you will bring sin upon yourselves, and if you pray, you will be condemned, and if you give to charity, you will harm your spirits. When you go into any region and walk through the countryside, when people receive you, eat what they serve you and heal the sick among them. For what goes into your mouth will not defile you; rather, it is what comes out of your mouth that will defile you.'"

5

Blessings on the Lion

[. . .] "Blessings on [the lion that a human eats, and the] lion will be [human. And cursed is the human] that [a lion eats . . .]." *(Greek Gospel of Thomas saying 7, in Papyrus Oxyrhynchus 654.40–42)*

Compare Gospel of Thomas saying 7: "Jesus said, 'Blessings on the lion that the human will eat, so that the lion becomes human. And foul is the human that the lion will eat, and the lion will become human.'"

THERE IS LIGHT WITHIN A PERSON OF LIGHT

"[. . .] There [is light within a person] of light, [and it shines on the whole] world. [If it does not shine, then] it is [dark]." *(Greek Gospel of Thomas saying 24, in Papyrus Oxyrhynchus 655[d].1–5)*

Compare Gospel of Thomas saying 24: "His followers said, 'Show us the place where you are, for we must seek it.' He said to them, 'Whoever has ears should hear. There is light within a person of light, and it shines on the whole world. If it does not shine, it is dark.'"

Take out the speck

IO

"[. . .] and then you will see clearly to take out the speck that is in your brother's eye." *(Greek Gospel of Thomas saying 26, in Papyrus Oxyrhynchus 1 [↓]. 1–4)*

———

Compare Gospel of Thomas saying 26: "Jesus said, 'You see the speck that is in your brother's eye, but you do not see the beam that is in your own eye. When you take the beam out of your own eye, then you will see clearly to take the speck out of your brother's eye.'"

If you do not fast from
the world

Jesus says, "If you do not fast from the world, you will not find God's kingdom. And if you do not observe the sabbath as a sabbath, you will not see the father." *(Greek Gospel of Thomas saying 27, in Papyrus Oxyrhynchus 1 [↓]. 4–11)*

I took my stand
in the midst of the world

Jesus says, "I took my stand in the midst of the world, and in flesh I appeared to them. I found them all drunk, and I found none of them thirsty. My soul aches for the children of humanity, because they are blind in their hearts and [do not] see [. . .]." *(Greek Gospel of Thomas saying 28, in Papyrus Oxyrhynchus 1 [↓]. 11–21)*

Compare Gospel of Thomas saying 28: "Jesus said, 'I took my stand in the midst of the world, and in flesh I appeared to them. I found them all drunk, and I did not find any of them thirsty. My soul ached for the children of humanity, because they are blind in their hearts and do not see, for they came into the world empty, and they also seek to depart from the world empty. But now they are drunk. When they shake off their wine, then they will repent.'"

Dwell in this poverty

"[. . . comes to dwell in this] poverty." *(Greek Gospel of Thomas saying 29, in Papyrus Oxyrhynchus 1 [→]. 22)*

Compare Gospel of Thomas saying 29: "Jesus said, 'If the flesh came into being because of spirit, it is a marvel, but if spirit came into being because of the body, it is a marvel of marvels. Yet I marvel at how this great wealth has come to dwell in this poverty.'"

Where there are three; lift up the stone

[Jesus says], "Where there are [three, they are without] God, and where there is only [one], I say, I am with that one.

"Lift up the stone, and you will find me there. Split the piece of wood, and I am there." *(Greek Gospel of Thomas sayings 30 and 77, in Papyrus Oxyrhynchus 1 [→]. 23–30)*

Compare Gospel of Thomas saying 30: "Jesus said, 'Where there are three deities, they are divine. Where there are two or one, I am with that one.'" Also compare Gospel of Thomas saying 77: "Jesus said, 'I am the light that is over all things. I am all: from me all has come forth, and to me all has reached. Split a piece of wood; I am there. Lift up the stone, and you will find me there.'"

A PROPHET IS NOT ACCEPTABLE

Jesus says, "A prophet is not acceptable in the prophet's own country, nor does a doctor perform healings on those who know the doctor." *(Greek Gospel of Thomas saying 31, in Papyrus Oxyrhynchus 1 [→]. 30–35)*

A CITY BUILT ON TOP
OF A HIGH HILL

Jesus says, "A city built on top of a high hill and fortified can neither fall nor be hidden." *(Greek Gospel of Thomas saying 32, in Papyrus Oxyrhynchus 1 [→]. 36–41)*

What you hear in one ear

Jesus says, "<What> you hear in one ear of yours, [proclaim . . .]." *(Greek Gospel of Thomas saying 33, in Papyrus Oxyrhynchus 1 [→]. 41–42)*

Compare Gospel of Thomas saying 33: "Jesus said, 'What you will hear in your ear, in the other ear proclaim from your rooftops. For no one lights a lamp and puts it under a basket, nor does one put it in a hidden place. Rather, one puts it on a stand so that all who come and go will see its light.'"

Do not worry

[Jesus says, "Do not worry], from morning [to evening nor] from evening [to] morning, either [about] your [food], what [you will] eat, [or] about [your clothing], what you [will] wear. [You are much] better than the lilies, which do not card or [spin]. As for you, when you have no garment, what [will you put] on? Who might add to your stature? That is the one who will give you your garment." *Greek Gospel of Thomas saying 36, in Papyrus Oxyrhynchus 655 col. i. 1–17)*

WHEN YOU STRIP AND ARE NOT ASHAMED

His followers say to him, "When will you be revealed to us, and when shall we see you?"

He says, "When you strip and are not ashamed, [. . . and you will not be afraid]." *(Greek Gospel of Thomas saying 37, in Papyrus Oxyrhynchus 655 col. i. 17–col. ii. 1)*

Compare Gospel of Thomas saying 37: "His followers said, 'When will you appear to us and when shall we see you?' Jesus said, 'When you strip without being ashamed and you take your clothes and put them under your feet like little children and trample them, then [you] will see the child of the living one and you will not be afraid.'"

You will seek me and not find me

[Jesus says, "Often you have desired to hear these sayings of mine], and [you have no one else from whom to hear (them)]. And [there will come days when you will seek me and you will not find me]." *(Greek Gospel of Thomas saying 38, in Papyrus Oxyrhynchus 655 col. ii. 2–11)*

The Pharisees and
the Scholars Have Taken
the Keys

[Jesus says, "The Pharisees and the scholars] have [taken the keys] of [knowledge; they themselves have] hidden [them. Neither] have [they] entered, [nor] have they [allowed those who are in the process of] entering [to enter. As for you, be as shrewd] as [snakes and as] innocent [as doves]." *(Greek Gospel of Thomas saying 39, in Papyrus Oxyrhynchus 655 col. ii. 11–23)*

ONE WHO SEEKS WILL FIND ME
IN CHILDREN

"One who seeks will find me in children from seven years, for there, hidden in the fourteenth age, I am revealed." *(Gospel of Thomas, in Hippolytus, Refutation of All Heresies 5.7.20)*

Compare Gospel of Thomas saying 4 and Unknown Saying 5 in this book.

IF YOU ATE DEAD THINGS

"If you ate dead things and made them living, what will you do if you eat living things?" *(Gospel of Thomas, in Hippolytus, Refutation of All Heresies 5.8.32)*

Compare Gospel of Thomas saying 11: "Jesus said, 'This heaven will pass away, and the one above it will pass away. The dead are not alive, and the living will not die. During the days when you ate what is dead, you made it alive. When you are in the light, what will you do? On the day when you were one, you became two. But when you become two, what will you do?' "

How have i sinned?

Look, the mother of the master and his brothers said to him, "John the Baptizer baptizes for the forgiveness of sins. Let us go and be baptized by him."

But he said to them, "How have I sinned, so that I should go and be baptized by him?—unless what I have said is ignorance." *(Gospel of the Hebrews [or Nazoreans] 2, in Jerome, Against the Pelagians 3.2)*

MY MOTHER THE HOLY SPIRIT

"Then my mother the holy spirit took me by one of my hairs and carried me to the great mount Tabor." *(Gospel of the Hebrews 4a, in Origen, Commentary on John 2)*

ONE WHO SEEKS WILL NOT STOP

"One who seeks will not stop until one finds. Having found, one will be astonished, and having been astonished, one will reign, and having reigned, one will rest." *(Gospel of the Hebrews 6b, in Clement of Alexandria, Miscellanies 5.14.96)*

Look at your brother with love

"And never be glad except when you look at your brother with love." *(Gospel of the Hebrews 7, in Jerome, Commentary on Ephesians 3)*

My brother James
the righteous

After the resurrection of the savior, it reports: now the master, when he had given the linen cloth to the priest's servant, went to James and appeared to him. For James had taken an oath that he would not eat bread from the hour that he drank of the master's cup until he would see him having risen from those who sleep.

And again, a little later: the master said, "Bring a table and bread."

And immediately it is added: he took the bread, blessed it, broke it, and gave it to James the Righteous, and said to him, "My brother, eat your bread, for the child of humankind has risen from those who sleep." *(Gospel of the Hebrews 9, in Jerome, On Famous Men 2)*

I CHOSE TWELVE APOSTLES

29

There was a certain man named Jesus who chose us, and he was about thirty years old. And when he came to Capernaum, he entered the house of Simon, who was nicknamed Peter, and he opened his mouth and said, "As I was walking by the lake of Tiberias, I chose John and James, sons of Zebedee, and Simon and Andrew and Thaddeus and Simon the Zealot and Judas Iscariot, and I called you, Matthew, while you were sitting at the tax booth, and you followed me. I want you, therefore, to be twelve apostles as a testimony to Israel." *(Gospel of the Ebionites 2, in Epiphanius, Panarion 30.13.2–3)*

My brothers and mother
and sisters

"Look, your mother and your brothers are standing outside."

"Who are my mother and brothers?"

And he pointed to his followers and said, "These are my brothers and mother and sisters, who do the will of my father." *(Gospel of the Ebionites 5, in Epiphanius, Panarion 30.14.5)*

I HAVE COME TO DO AWAY
WITH SACRIFICES

"I have come to do away with sacrifices, and if you do not stop sacrificing, the wrath will not stop from among you." *(Gospel of the Ebionites 6, in Epiphanius, Panarion 30.16.5)*

I DO NOT DESIRE TO EAT MEAT

(The followers:) "Where do you want us to prepare things for you to eat the Passover meal?"

(Jesus:) "I certainly do not desire to eat meat with you at this Passover, do I?" *(Gospel of the Ebionites 7, in Epiphanius, Panarion 30.22.4)*

The lord's prayer:
our bread for tomorrow

In the so-called Gospel of the Hebrews, instead of "the bread for our existence," I (Jerome) found "*mahar*," which means "for tomorrow," so that the sense is "Give us today our bread for tomorrow," that is, for the future. *(Gospel of the Nazoreans 3a, in Jerome, Commentary on Matthew 1)*

Compare Matthew 6:9–13 (Q): "Our father in heaven, may your name be holy. May your kingdom come, may your will be done on earth as it is in heaven. Give us today our bread we need for the day. And forgive us our debts, as we also have forgiven those in debt to us. And do not lead us to the test, but deliver us from the evil one"; Luke 11:2–4 (Q): "Father, may your name be holy. May your kingdom come. Give us each day our bread we need for the day. And forgive us our sins, for we ourselves forgive everyone in debt to us. And do not lead us to the test."

He said, "If your brother has sinned with a word and has made amends with you, welcome him seven times a day."

His follower Simon said to him, "Seven times a day?"

The master answered and said to him, "In fact, I tell you, as often as seventy times seven times. For in the prophets also, after they were anointed with the holy spirit, sinful language was found." *(Gospel of the Nazoreans 5, in Jerome, Against the Pelagians 3.2)*

Go sell everything
that you own

The other rich man said to him, "Teacher, what good must I do to live?"

He said to him, "Mister, do what is in the law and the prophets."

He answered him, "I have done that."

He said to him, "Go sell everything that you own, distribute it to the poor, and come follow me."

But the rich man began to scratch his head, and he was not pleased about this. And the master said to him, "How can you say, 'I have done what is in the law and the prophets'? For it is written in the law, 'Love your neighbor as yourself.' And look, many of your brothers, sons of Abraham, are covered with filth and dying of hunger, but your house is full of many good things, and not a single thing comes out of it for them."

And he turned and said to his follower Simon, who was sitting by him, "Simon, son of Jonah, it is easier for a camel to go through a needle's eye than for a rich person to enter heaven's kingdom." *(Gospel of the Nazoreans 6, in Origen, Commentary on Matthew 15.14)*

Parable of the money entrusted to servants: another version

The gospel that has come down to us in Hebrew letters does not direct the threat against the person who hid (the money) but rather against the person who lived a debauched life, for he (the master) had three servants, one who squandered the master's property with whores and flute girls, one who multiplied the earnings, and one who hid the money; so one was commended, one was merely criticized, and one was locked up in prison. *(Gospel of the Nazoreans 8, in Eusebius, Theophany 4.22)*

———

Compare Matthew 24:45–51 and 25:14–30. In the former passage, Jesus describes a servant abusing fellow servants and living a debauched life and then being punished; in the latter passage, which presents the parable of the money entrusted to servants, Jesus describes a master praising two servants who multiplied the master's money and condemning a servant who hid the master's money.

I CHOOSE THE MOST WORTHY

37

"I choose for myself the most worthy: the most worthy are the ones whom my heavenly father has given me." *(Gospel of the Nazoreans 11, in Eusebius, Theophany 4.12)*

IF YOU ARE IN MY EMBRACE

"If you are in my embrace and do not do the will of my father in heaven, I shall cast you away from me." *(Gospel of the Nazoreans [?], in Codex 1424 [Zion gospel edition])*

AS LONG AS WOMEN BEAR CHILDREN

When Salome asked, "How long will death prevail?" the master answered, "As long as you women bear children," not as if life were bad and creation evil, but so as to teach the order of nature, for death always follows birth. *(Gospel of the Egyptians 1a, in Clement of Alexandria, Miscellanies 3.6.45)*

Do not eat the plant that has bitterness

For when she (Salome) said, "So I have done well not to have borne children," as if it were improper to engage in procreation, the master answered and said, "Eat every plant, but do not eat the one that has bitterness." *(Gospel of the Egyptians 2, in Clement of Alexandria, Miscellanies 3.9.66)*

When you have trampled the garment of shame

When Salome inquired when the things about which she had asked would be known, the master said, "When you have trampled the garment of shame, and when the two become one, and the male with the female is neither male nor female." *(Gospel of the Egyptians 3, in Clement of Alexandria, Miscellanies 3.13.92)*

Do away with the works of the female

The savior himself said, "I have come to do away with the works of the female," by "female" meaning lust and by "works" birth and death. *(Gospel of the Egyptians 4, in Clement of Alexandria, Miscellanies 3.9.63)*

Do not fear the wolves

"Hear me, you lambs whom I have chosen, and do not fear the wolves." *(Gospel of the Egyptians [?], in Pseudo-Titus, Epistle 1)*

Brother thomas, listen to me

The hidden sayings that the savior spoke to Judas Thomas, that I, Mathaias, in turn recorded. I was walking, listening to them speak with each other.

The savior said, "Brother Thomas, while you are still in the world, listen to me and I shall reveal to you what you have thought about in your heart." *(Book of Thomas 138,1–7)*

You are the person who knows himself

"Now since it is said that you are my twin and my true friend, examine yourself and understand who you are, how you exist, and how you will come to be. Since you are to be called my brother, it is not fitting for you to be ignorant of yourself. And I know that you have understood, for already you have understood that I am the knowledge of truth. So while you are walking with me, though you are ignorant, already you have obtained knowledge, and you will be called the person who knows himself. For one who has not known oneself has not known anything, but one who has known oneself already has acquired knowledge about the depth of the universe. So then, my brother Thomas, you have seen what is hidden from people, what they stumble against in their ignorance." *(Book of Thomas 138,7–21)*

You are students

The savior answered and said, "If what is visible to you is obscure to you, how can you comprehend what is invisible? If the deeds of truth that are visible in the world are difficult for you to accomplish, how then will you accomplish things pertaining to the exalted greatness and the fullness, which are invisible? How then will you be called workers? For this reason you are students and have not yet attained the greatness of perfection." *(Book of Thomas 138,27–36)*

You are children

"So, then, you are children until you become perfect." *(Book of Thomas 139,11–12)*

LIGHT DWELLS IN LIGHT

Jesus said, "It is in the light that the light dwells."*(Book of Thomas 139,21–22)*

TEACHING FOR THE PERFECT

Again the savior answered and said, "This is why we must speak to you, because this is the teaching for those who are perfect. So if you wish to become perfect, you will keep these (sayings). If not, the name for you is 'ignorant,' since an intelligent person cannot associate with a fool, for the intelligent person is perfect in all wisdom. To the fool, however, good and evil are one and the same. For the wise person will be nourished by truth, and will be like a tree growing by the stream of water." *(Book of Thomas 140,8–18)*

Blessings on the wise person who has sought truth

[The savior] answered and said, "[Blessings] on the wise person who has [sought truth, and] when it has been found, has rested upon it forever, and has not been afraid of those who wish to trouble him." *(Book of Thomas 140, 40–141,2)*

Story of plant life

The savior answered, "Listen to what I shall say to you and believe in the truth. What sows and what is sown will pass away in their fire, in fire and water, and will be hidden in tombs of darkness. And after a long time the fruit of evil trees will appear and will be punished and slain in the mouths of animals and people, through the agency of the rains, the winds, the air, and the light shining above." *(Book of Thomas 142,9–18)*

THE DAY OF JUDGMENT

The savior answered and said, "[In] truth I say to you, whoever listens to [your] word and turns away, or sneers at it, or smirks at these things, in truth I say to you, that person will be handed over to the ruler who is on high, who rules as king over all the powers, and the ruler will make that person turn away, and will cast that one down from on high into the abyss, and that one will be imprisoned in a cramped, dark place. So that person cannot turn or move because of the great depth of Tartaros and the burdensome [bitterness] of Hades. Whoever relies on what [is brought] to him [. . .] will not be forgiven [his madness], but will [be judged. Whoever has] persecuted you will be handed over to the angel Tartarouchos, [who has flaming] fire that pursues them, and fiery whips that spew forth sparks into the face of one who is pursued. If one flees to the west, one finds fire. If one turns south, one finds it there as well. If one turns north, the threat of erupting fire meets one again. Nor does one find the way to the east, to flee there and be saved, for that person did not find it while embodied so as to find it on the day of judgment." *(Book of Thomas 142,26–143,7)*

ALAS FOR YOU GODLESS PEOPLE

Then the savior continued and said, "Alas for you godless people, who have no hope, who are secure in things that will not happen.

"Alas for you who hope in the flesh and in the prison that will perish. . . .

"Alas for you with the fire that burns within you, for it is insatiable.

"Alas for you because of the wheel that turns in your minds.

"Alas for you because of the smoldering that is within you. . . .

"Alas for you prisoners, for you are bound in caves. . . .

"Alas for you who dwell in error. . . .

"Alas for you who love intercourse and filthy association with the female.

"And alas for you because of the powers of your bodies, for they will mistreat you.

"Alas for you because of the actions of the evil demons.

"Alas for you who entice your limbs with fire. . . ."
(Book of Thomas 143,8–144,14)

Parable of the grapevine and the weeds

"The sun and the moon will give a fragrant aroma to you, as will the air, the spirit, the earth, and the water. For if the sun does not shine upon these bodies, they will rot and perish just like a weed or grass. If the sun shines upon it, it becomes strong and chokes the grapevine. But if the grapevine becomes strong, and casts its shadow over the weeds and all the rest of the brush growing with it, and [spreads] and fills out, it alone inherits the land where it grows, and dominates wherever it has cast its shadow. So then, when it grows, it dominates the whole land, and it is productive for its master and pleases him greatly, for he would have gone to great pains because of the weeds before pulling them out, but the grapevine by itself has disposed of them and choked them, and they have died and have become like earth." *(Book of Thomas 144,19–36)*

BLESSINGS ON YOU WHO UNDERSTAND BEFOREHAND

Then Jesus continued and said to them, "Alas for [you], for you have not learned the teaching. . . .

"Blessings on you who understand beforehand the temptations and who flee from things that are alien.

"Blessings on you who are mocked and are not respected because of the love your master has for you.

"Blessings on you who cry and are oppressed by those who have no hope, for you will be released from all bondage." *(Book of Thomas 144,36–145,8)*

WATCH, PRAY, REST, REIGN

"Watch and pray that you may not come to be in the flesh, but that you may leave the bondage of the bitterness of this life. And when you pray, you will find rest, for you have left pain and reproach behind. For when you leave the pains and the passions of the body, you will receive rest from the good one, and you will reign with the king, you united with him and he united with you, from now on, forever and ever. Amen." *(Book of Thomas 145,8–16)*

LEAVE OUR LABOR BEHIND AND REST

The savior said to his followers, "Now the moment has come, brothers, for us to leave our labor behind and stand at rest. For whoever stands at rest will rest forever." *(Dialogue of the Savior 1)*

I OPENED THE WAY

"But when I came, I opened the way and taught them about the bridge that they will cross, those who are chosen and alone, [who] have known the father, since they have believed the truth, and all the praises <with which> you give praise." *(Dialogue of the Savior 1)*

When you give praise

"So when you give praise, do it like this: Hear us, father, as you have heard your only son and have accepted him [and] have given him rest from many [labors]. . . . You are [the] thought and all the tranquillity of those who are alone. Again, hear us, as you have heard those who are your chosen ones, those <who>, through your sacrifice, will enter by means of their good deeds, whose souls have been saved from these blind limbs, so that they might exist forever. Amen." *(Dialogue of the Savior 2)*

Truth seeks the wise

"For truth seeks the wise and the righteous." *(Dialogue of the Savior 7)*

THE LAMP OF THE BODY

The savior [said], "The lamp [of the] body is the mind. As long as [what is within] you is in good order, that is, [the soul], your bodies are [enlightened]. As long as your hearts are dark, your light that you anticipate [is far from you]. I have called [you to myself], since I am about to depart, so that [you may receive] my word among [yourselves. Look], I am sending it to [you]." *(Dialogue of the Savior 8)*

Compare Matthew 6:22–23 (Q): "The lamp of the body is the eye. If, then, your eye is clear, your whole body will be bright, but if eye is evil, your whole body will be dark. So if the light within you is darkness, how intense is the darkness!"; Luke 11:34–35 (Q): "The lamp of the body is your eye. When your eye is clear, your whole body is bright, but when it is evil, your body is dark. Watch out, then, that the light within you not be darkness."

The one who seeks also reveals

62

His followers [said, "Master], who is the one who seeks and [who is the one who] reveals?"

[The master] said [to them], "The one who seeks [is also the one who] reveals."

[Matthew said to him again, "Master], when I [listen to you] and when I speak, who is the one who [speaks and who is] the one who listens?"

The [master] said, "The one who speaks is also the one who [listens], and the one who sees is also the one who reveals." *(Dialogue of the Savior 9–12)*

What you seek is within

"And [in truth] I say to you, what you seek [and] inquire after, look, [it is] within you. . . ." *(Dialogue of the Savior 16)*

If a person sets his soul on high

"If a person sets [his] soul on high, then [that person will] be exalted." *(Dialogue of the Savior 18)*

Let one who has power renounce it

65

"I say to you, let one [who has] power renounce [it and repent], and [let] one who [knows] seek and find and rejoice." *(Dialogue of the Savior 20)*

Everyone who has known oneself has seen

66

Matthew said, "Master, I want [to see] that place of life, where there is no wickedness, but it is pure light."

The master said, "Brother Matthew, you will not be able to see it as [long as you] are wearing flesh."

Matthew said, "Master, even [if I will] not [be able to] see it, let me [know about it]."

The master said, "Everyone who has known oneself has seen oneself. Everything that person is given to do that person does. So such a person has come to [resemble] that place in goodness." *(Dialogue of the Savior 27–30)*

IF ONE DOES NOT STAND
IN THE DARKNESS

"Whoever does [not] know [the] work of perfection does not [know] anything. If one does not stand in the darkness, one will not be able to see the light." *(Dialogue of the Savior 34)*

UNDERSTAND HOW ONE HAS COME

"Whoever will not understand how one has come will not understand how one will go, and that person is not a stranger to this world, which will [exalt itself and] be humbled." *(Dialogue of the Savior 35)*

YOU WILL DOMINATE THE RULERS

Judas said, "Look, the rulers dwell above us, so it is they who will dominate us."

The master said, "It is you who will dominate them. But when you remove ill will from yourselves, then you will clothe yourselves with light and enter the wedding chamber." *(Dialogue of the Savior 49–50)*

Fullness and deficiency

The followers said to him, "What is fullness and what is deficiency?"

He said to them, "You are from fullness and you dwell in the place where there is deficiency. And look, his (or its) light has flowed down upon me." *(Dialogue of the Savior 54–55)*

Eye has not seen

Matthew said, "Tell me, master, how the dead die [and] how the living live."

The master said, "[You have] asked me about a [true] saying that eye has not seen nor have I heard it except from you. But I say to you, when what animates a person is removed, that person will be called dead, and when what is living leaves what is dead, it will be called alive." *(Dialogue of the Savior 56–57)*

Compare Gospel of Thomas saying 17: "Jesus said, 'I shall give you what no eye has seen, what no ear has heard, what no hand has touched, what has not arisen in the human heart.'"

Whoever is from the female dies

Judas said, "Why, then, in truth, do some die and some live?"

The master said, "Whoever is from truth does not die; whoever is from the female dies." *(Dialogue of the Savior 58–59)*

THIS WORLD'S GOLD AND SILVER

Mary said, "I want to understand all things, [as] they are."

The [master] said, "One who will seek life—this indeed is their wealth. For this world's [pleasure (or rest)] is [a lie], and its gold and its silver are [a] deception." *(Dialogue of the Savior 69–70)*

THE BEGINNING OF THE WAY

Judas said, "Tell me, master, what is the beginning of the way?"

He said, "Love and goodness. For if one of these had existed among the rulers, wickedness would never have come to be." *(Dialogue of the Savior 73–74)*

You will be blessed when you strip yourselves

Judas said to Matthew, "We want to understand with what sort of garments we shall be clothed when we emerge from the corruption of the [flesh]."

The master said, "The rulers [and] the officials have garments that are given only for a time and that do not last. [But] you, as children of truth, are not to clothe yourselves with these garments that are only for a time. Rather, I say to you, you will be blessed when you strip yourselves." *(Dialogue of the Savior 84–85)*

The mother of all

Mary said, "[Of what] sort is this mustard seed? Is it from heaven or is it from earth?"

The master said, "When the father established the world for himself, he left many things with the mother of all. For this reason he sows and works." *(Dialogue of the Savior 88–89)*

Pray in a place where there is no female

Judas said, "You have told us this from the mind of truth. When we pray, how should we pray?"

The master said, "Pray in a place where there is no female."

Matthew said, "He tells us, 'Pray in a place where there is [no female],' meaning, 'Destroy the works of the female,' not because there is any other [birth] but because they will stop [giving birth]." *(Dialogue of the Savior 90–92)*

BE CONFIDENT OF HEART

"For this reason I said to you, be confident of heart, and if you lack confidence, be confident before the different forms of nature. Whoever has ears to hear should hear." *(Gospel of Mary 8,6–11)*

The child of humankind
is within

When the blessed one had said this, he greeted all of them and said, "Peace be with you. Take my peace to yourselves.

"Watch out that no one mislead you by saying, 'Look, here,' or, 'Look, there,' for the child of humankind is within you. Follow him. Those who seek him will find him." *(Gospel of Mary 8,11–21)*

Do not lay down any rule

"Go, then, and preach the good news of the kingdom. Do not lay down any rule beyond what I have set for you, and do not establish a law like the lawmaker, or you will be bound by it." *(Gospel of Mary 8,21–9,4)*

Blessings on you, mary

Peter said to Mary, "Sister, we know that the savior loved you more than any other woman. Tell us the words of the savior that you remember, that you know but we do not, nor have we heard them."

Mary answered and said, "What is hidden from you I shall relate to you."

And she began to speak these words to them: "As for me," she said, "I saw the master in a vision and I said to him, 'Master, today I saw you in a vision.' He answered and said to me, 'Blessings on you for not wavering at seeing me. For where the mind is, there is the treasure.'" *(Gospel of Mary 10,1–16)*

Take nothing from the father's house

The master said to the followers, "[Take something] from every house and bring it into the father's house, but do not seize anything in the father's house and carry it away." *(Gospel of Philip 55,37–56,3)*

Unite the angels with us

He said on that day, in the prayer of thanksgiving, "You who have united the perfect light with the holy spirit, unite the angels also with us, the images." *(Gospel of Philip 58,10–14)*

ASK YOUR MOTHER

Because of this, one day a follower asked the master for something of the world. He said to the person, "Ask your mother, and she will give you something from another realm." *(Gospel of Philip 59,23–27)*

THE CHILD OF HUMANKIND
AS A DYER

The master entered Levi's dyehouse. He took seventy-two colors and threw them into the vat. He took them out, and they were all white. And he said, "In this way has the child of humankind come [as] a dyer." *(Gospel of Philip 63,25–30)*

Loving mary of magdala

86

And [the] companion of the [savior is] Mary of Magdala. The [savior loved her] more than [all] the followers, [and he] kissed her often on her [mouth]. The rest of [the followers . . .]. They said to him, "Why do you love her more than all of us?"

The savior answered and said to them, "Why do I not love you like her? When a blind person and one who can see are both together in darkness, they are no different from each other. When the light comes, then one who can see will see the light and one who is blind will stay in darkness." *(Gospel of Philip 63,32–64,9)*

BLESSINGS ON ONE WHO
EXISTS BEFORE

The master said, "Blessings on one who exists before coming into being. For one who exists has been and will be." *(Gospel of Philip 64,9–12)*

WHAT IS BELOW LIKE WHAT
IS ABOVE

He said, "I have come to make [what is] below like what is [above and what is] outside like what is [inside, and to unite] them in [that] place." *(Gospel of Philip 67,30–34)*

Some have entered laughing

The master said very well, "Some have entered heaven's kingdom laughing, and they have left [laughing]." *(Gospel of Philip 74,24–27)*

I shall return

And five hundred fifty days after he rose from the dead, we said to him, "Did you depart and leave us?"

Jesus said, "No, but I shall return to the place from which I have come. If you want to come with me, come."

They all answered and said, "If you order us, we shall come."

He said, "In truth I say to you, no one will ever enter

heaven's kingdom because I ordered it, but rather because you yourselves are filled. Leave James and Peter to me, that I may fill them." *(Secret Book of James 2,19–35)*

You have seen the child of humankind

"From now on, while awake or asleep, remember that you have seen the child of humankind, and have spoken with him, and have listened to him.

"Alas for those who have seen the child [of] humankind.

"Blessings will be on you who have not seen that person, and have not associated with him, and have not spoken with him, and have not listened to anything from him: yours is life.

"So understand that he healed you when you were sick, that you might reign.

"Alas for those who have found relief from their sickness, for they will relapse into sickness.

"Blessings on you who have not been sick, and have known relief before getting sick: God's kingdom is yours.

"For this reason I say to you, be filled and leave no space within you empty, or the one who is coming will be able to mock you." *(Secret Book of James 3,11–38)*

BE FILLED WITH THE SPIRIT

"So be filled with the spirit but lacking in reason, for reason is of the soul; in fact, it is soul." *(Secret Book of James 4,18–22)*

IF YOU ARE OPPRESSED BY SATAN

I answered and said to him, "Master, we can obey you if you wish, for we have forsaken our fathers and our mothers and our villages, and have followed you. Give us, then, the means not to be tempted by the evil devil."

The master answered and said, "What merit is it to you if you do the father's will but you are not given from him what he gives, as a part of his bounty, when you are tempted by Satan? But if you are oppressed by Satan and persecuted, and you do his (the father's) will, I [say], he will love you, and make you my equal, and consider you to have become beloved through his forethought, by your own choice. So will you not stop loving the flesh and being afraid of sufferings? Or do you not know that you have not yet been abused and you have not yet been unjustly accused, nor have you yet been locked up in prison, nor have you yet been unlawfully condemned, nor have you yet been crucified <without> reason, nor have you yet been buried in the sand, as I myself was, by the evil one? Do you dare to spare the flesh, O you for whom the spirit is a wall surrounding you? If you consider how long the world has existed <before> you and how long it will exist after you, you will discover that your life is but a single day and your sufferings but a single hour. For the good will not enter the world. Disdain death, then, and care about life. Remember my cross and my death, and you will live." *(Secret Book of James 4,22–5,35)*

BE LIKE THE CHILD OF THE HOLY SPIRIT

And I answered and said to him, "Master, do not mention to us the cross and death, for they are far from you."

The master answered and said, "In truth I say to you, none will be saved unless they believe in my cross, [for] God's kingdom belongs to those who have believed in my cross. Be seekers of death, then, like the dead who seek life, for what they seek becomes apparent to them. And what is there to cause them concern? As for you, when you search out death, it will teach you about being chosen. In truth I say to you, none of those who are afraid of death will be saved, for death's (or <God's>) kingdom belongs to those who are put (or put themselves) to death. Become better than I; be like the child of the holy spirit." *(Secret Book of James 5,35–6,21)*

THE HEAD OF PROPHECY
WAS CUT OFF

Then I asked him, "Master, how shall we be able to prophesy to those who ask us to prophesy to them? For there are many who bring a request to us, and look to us to hear a pronouncement from us."

The master answered and said, "Do you not know that the head of prophecy was cut off with John?"

But I said, "Master, it is not possible to remove the head of prophecy, is it?"

The master said to me, "When you realize what 'head' means, and that prophecy comes from the head, then understand the meaning of 'its head was removed.'

"First I spoke with you in parables, and you did not understand. Now I am speaking with you openly, and you do not perceive. Nevertheless, you were for me a parable among parables and a disclosure among things revealed." *(Secret Book of James 6,21–7,10)*

Outdo me

"Be eager to be saved without being urged. Rather, be fervent on your own and, if possible, outdo even me, for this is how the father will love you." *(Secret Book of James 7,10–16)*

Hate hypocrisy

97

"Come to hate hypocrisy and evil intention, for it is intention that produces hypocrisy, and hypocrisy is far from truth." *(Secret Book of James 7,17–22)*

Parable of the date palm shoot

98

"Do not let heaven's kingdom wither away. For it is like a palm shoot whose dates dropped around it. It produced buds, and after they grew, its productivity was made to dry up. This is also what happened with the fruit that came from this single root. After it was harvested, fruit was obtained by many. It certainly would be good if you could produce new growth now. You would find it." *(Secret Book of James 7,22–35)*

Parable of the Grain of Wheat

"Be eager about the word. For the first aspect of the word is faith, the second is love, the third is works, and from these comes life.

"For the word is like a grain of wheat. When someone sowed it, he had faith in it, and when it sprouted, he loved it, because he saw many grains instead of just one. And after he worked, he was saved, because he prepared it as food, and he still kept some out to sow.

"This is also how you can acquire heaven's kingdom for yourselves. Unless you acquire it through knowledge, you will not be able to find it." *(Secret Book of James 8,10–27)*

100

"For this reason I say to you, be sober. Do not go astray. And often have I said to you all together, and also to you alone, James, have I said, be saved. And I have commanded you to follow me, and I have taught you how to speak before the rulers.

"See that I have come down and have spoken and have exerted myself and have won my crown, when I saved you. For I came down to dwell with you, that you might also dwell with me. And when I found that your houses had no roofs, I dwelled in houses that could receive me at the time that I came down." *(Secret Book of James 8,27–9,9)*

THE FATHER DOES NOT NEED ME

"Therefore, trust in me, O my brothers. Understand what the great light is. The father does not need me, for a father does not need a son, but it is the son who needs the father. To him I am going, for the father of the son is not in need of you." *(Secret Book of James 9,9–18)*

LOVE LIFE

"Listen to the word, understand knowledge, love life, and no one will persecute you and no one will oppress you, other than you yourselves." *(Secret Book of James 9,18–23)*

You wretches

103

"O you wretches! O you poor devils! O you pretenders to truth! O you falsifiers of knowledge! O you sinners against the spirit! Do you still dare to listen when from the beginning you should have been speaking? Do you still dare to sleep when from the beginning you should have been awake, so that heaven's kingdom might receive you? In truth I say to you, it is easier for a holy person to sink into defilement, and for an enlightened person to sink into darkness, than for you to reign—or not to reign." *(Secret Book of James 9,24–10,6)*

If i had been sent to those who would listen

104

"In truth I say to you, if I had been sent to those who would listen to me and had spoken with them, I would never have come down to earth. From now on, then, be ashamed for these things." *(Secret Book of James 10,15–21)*

Blessings on one who has seen you

105

"Look, I shall be leaving you and shall go away, and I do not want to stay with you any longer, just as you yourselves have not wanted this. Now, then, follow me quickly. For this reason I say to you, for your sakes I came down. You are loved ones; you are the ones who will be the cause of life for many people. Invoke the father, pray to God frequently, and he will give unto you.

"Blessings on one who has seen you with him when he is proclaimed among the angels and glorified among the saints: yours is life. Rejoice and be glad as children of God. Observe [his] will, that you may be saved. Accept correction from me, and save yourselves. I am mediating for you with the father, and he will forgive you many things." *(Secret Book of James 10,22–11,6)*

COMPARE YOURSELVES
TO FOREIGNERS

"Alas for you who are in need of an advocate.

"Alas for you who stand in need of grace.

"Blessings will be on those who have spoken out and have acquired grace for themselves.

"Compare yourselves to foreigners. How are they viewed in your city? Why are you anxious to banish yourselves on your own and distance yourselves from your city? Why abandon your dwelling on your own and make it available for those who want to live in it? O you exiles and runaways, alas for you, for you will be captured." *(Secret Book of James 11,11–29)*

A FOURTH ONE IN HEAVEN

107

"In truth I say to you, he (God) will never forgive the sin of the soul or the guilt of the flesh, for none of those who have worn the flesh will be saved. So do you think that many have found heaven's kingdom?

"Blessings on one who has seen oneself as a fourth one in heaven." *(Secret Book of James 12,9–17)*

Parable of the Head of Grain

108

"For this reason I say this to you, that you may know yourselves.

"For heaven's kingdom is like a head of grain that sprouted in a field. And when it was ripe, it scattered its seed, and again it filled the field with heads of grain for another year.

"So also with you, be eager to harvest for yourselves a head of the grain of life, that you may be filled with the kingdom." *(Secret Book of James 12,20–31)*

BLESSINGS ON THOSE WHO HAVE NOT SEEN BUT HAVE BELIEVED

109

"And as long as I am with you, pay attention to me and trust in me, but when I am far from you, remember me. And remember me because I was with you and you did not know me.

"Blessings will be on those who have known me.

"Alas for those who have heard and have not believed.

"Blessings will be on those who have not seen but [have believed]." *(Secret Book of James 12,31–13,1)*

IIO

"And once again I appeal to you. For I am disclosed to you as I am building a house that is very useful to you when you find shelter in it, just as it will be able to support (or stand alongside) your neighbors' house when theirs threatens [to] collapse.

"In truth I say to you, alas for those for whom I was sent down to this place.

"Blessings will be on those who are going up to the father.

"Again I admonish you, O you who exist. Be like those who do not exist, that you may dwell with those who do not exist." *(Secret Book of James 13,2–17)*

Do not let heaven's kingdom become a desert

III

"Do not let heaven's kingdom become a desert within you. Do not be proud because of the light that enlightens. Rather, act toward yourselves as I myself have toward you. I have put myself under a curse for you, that you might be saved." *(Secret Book of James 13,17–25)*

Whoever will believe in the kingdom will never leave it

II2

"In truth I say to you, whoever will receive life and believe in the kingdom will never leave it, not even if the father wants to banish him." *(Secret Book of James 14,14–19)*

I SHALL STRIP AND CLOTHE MYSELF

113

"For today I must take my place at the right hand of my father. I have spoken my last word to you; I shall depart from you, for a chariot of spirit has lifted me up, and from now on I shall strip myself that I may clothe myself.

"So pay attention: blessings on those who have proclaimed the son before he came down, so that, when I did come, I might ascend.

"Blessings three times over on those who [were] proclaimed by the son before they came into being, so that you might share with them." *(Secret Book of James 14,30–15,5)*

Salted with salt

114

"And every sacrifice will be salted with salt." *(Replaces or follows Mark 9:49 in several manuscripts)*

Compare Mark 9:49: "For everyone will be salted with fire."

Seek to increase from what is little

115

"But as for you, seek to increase from what is little and (not) to become less from what is greater. When you go into a place and are invited to dine, do not recline in the places of honor, or someone more distinguished than you might arrive and the host might come over and say to you, 'Move further down,' and you would be humiliated. But if you sit down in a less important place and someone less important than you arrives, the host will say to you, 'Join us further up,' and this will be to your advantage." *(Follows Matthew 20:28 in Codex Bezae and other manuscripts)*

IF YOU KNOW WHAT YOU ARE DOING

116

On the same day he saw someone working on the sabbath and he said to him, "Mister, if you know what you are doing, you are blessed, but if you do not know, you are damned and you are a lawbreaker." *(Follows Luke 6:4 in Codex Bezae)*

Not to destroy but to save

And he said, "You do not know of what spirit you are, for the child of humankind has not come to destroy human lives but to save them." *(Follows Luke 9:55 in several manuscripts)*

Show mercy

Let us especially remember the words of the master Jesus, which he spoke when he was teaching considerateness and patience. For he spoke in this way: "Show mercy, that you may be shown mercy. Forgive, that you may be forgiven. As you do to others, so will it be done to you. As you give, so will it be given to you. As you judge, so will you be judged. As you show kindness, so will kindness be shown to you. The standard you use will be used back on you." *(1 Clement 13:1–2)*

Bless those who curse you

119

The way of life is this: first, you shall love God who made you, and second, your neighbor as yourself. And whatever you do not want to be done to you, do not do to someone else.

The teaching of these words is this: bless those who curse you, and pray for your enemies, and fast for those who persecute you. For what merit is it to you if you love those who love you? Do not even the pagans do this? But you, love those who hate you, and you will have no enemy. Keep away from fleshly and bodily lusts. If someone slaps you on the right cheek, turn to that person the other also, and you will be perfect. If someone forces you to go one mile, go with that person two. If someone takes your outer garment, give that person your undergarment also. If someone takes from you what is yours, do not demand it back—for you cannot, anyway. Give to everyone who asks of you, and do not demand repayment, for the father wishes that to all people there be given from his own gifts. Blessings on one who gives according to the commandment, for that person is guiltless. Alas for one who receives, for if someone receives when needy, that person is guiltless, but someone who is not needy will stand trial concerning why that person received and for what purpose, and while in detention his actions will be investigated, and he will not get out from there until he has paid back the last cent. But it has also been said concerning this, Let your donation sweat in your hands, until you know to whom to give it. *(Didache 1:2–6)*

PRAY FOR YOUR ENEMIES

"And pray for your enemies. For one who is not [against] you is for you. [One who] is far away [today] will be [near you] tomorrow. . . ." *(Papyrus Oxyrhynchus 1224, p. 176)*

SEARCH THE SCRIPTURES

121

[And Jesus said] to the lawyers, "[Punish] everyone who breaks [the] law and not me, [for a lawbreaker does not know] how he is doing what he is doing."

[And turning] to [the] rulers of the people, he spoke this saying: "Search the scriptures, in which you think that you have life. It is they [that] give evidence about me. Do not [suppose] that I have come to accuse [you] to my father. [The one who] accuses you is Moses, in whom you have trusted."

When they [said], "We know very well that God spoke to Moses, but as for you, we do not know [where you are from]," Jesus answered and said to [them], "Now [you] are accused for [not] trusting what is [testified] by him. For if [you] had [trusted Moses], you would have trusted [me], for he [wrote about] me to your ancestors." *(Papyrus Egerton 2, 1 verso, 1–23)*

Why do you call me teacher?

122

[Coming] to him, they tested him by questioning him, and [said], "Teacher Jesus, we know that you have come [from God], for what you do gives [evidence] beyond all the prophets. [Tell] us, [then], is it permitted to [pay] the kings what is due to them? [Should we] pay them or not?"

But Jesus knew [their] intention and, [being] indignant, he said to [them], "Why do you call me teacher [with] your mouth without [hearing] what I say? [Isaiah] prophesied rightly [about] you when he said, 'This [people honors] me with their [lips, but] their [heart] is [far] from [me. In] vain [they worship me, teaching human] commandments [. . .]'" (Isaiah 29:13). *(Papyrus Egerton 2, 2 recto, 43–59)*

Compare Gospel of Thomas saying 100: "They showed Jesus a gold coin and said to him, 'Caesar's people demand taxes from us.' He said to them, 'Give Caesar the things that are Caesar's, give God the things that are God's, and give me what is mine'"; longer versions in Mark 12:13–17, Matthew 22:15–22, and Luke 20:20–26.

You have cleansed yourself in the water of dogs and pigs

123

And he took them (the followers) and led them into the place of purity itself, and he was walking about in the temple.

And a certain Pharisee, a chief priest named Levi, approached and met them, and [said] to the savior, "Who gave you permission to walk around in this place of purity and look upon [these] holy vessels when you have not cleansed yourself, and your followers have not even washed their [feet]? Rather, while defiled, you have walked around in this temple, which is a ritually clean [place], in which no one walks around [or dares to look upon these] holy vessels [without] having cleansed oneself and having changed clothes."

And [immediately the savior stood, with] the followers, and answered him, "Then you, who are here in the temple, are clean?"

He says to him, "I am clean, for I have cleansed myself in David's pool, and I have gone down by one set of steps and have come up by the other, and I have put on clean white clothes, and then I came and looked upon these holy vessels."

The savior answered and said to him, "Alas for you blind people who do not see. You have cleansed yourself in these stagnant waters in which dogs and pigs have wallowed night and day, and you have washed and wiped clean the outer layer of skin that whores and flute girls [also] anoint and wash and wipe clean [and] beautify for the lust of men, but within they are filled with scorpions and wickedness [of every sort]. Yet I and [my followers], whom you say are unwashed, [have been] washed in living waters (or waters [of eternal] life), which come down from [heaven (?)]. But alas for those [. . .]." *(Papyrus Oxyrhynchus 840)*

Compare Matthew 7:6: "Do not give what is holy to dogs; and do not throw your pearls before pigs, or they might trample them under foot and turn and maul you"; Gospel of Thomas saying 93: "Do not give what is holy to dogs, or they might throw them upon the manure pile. Do not throw pearls [to] pigs, or they might make [mud] of it."

Not everyone will be saved

For he says, "Not everyone who says to me, 'Master, master,' will be saved, but whoever does righteousness."
(2 Clement 4:2)

Be as lambs among wolves

For the master says, "You will be as lambs among wolves."

But Peter answers and says to him, "Then what if the wolves tear the lambs apart?"

Jesus said to Peter, "The lambs should not be afraid of the wolves after their death. And you, do not be afraid of those who kill you and can do nothing more to you.

Rather, be afraid of the one who, after your death, has power over soul and body, to cast them into fiery hell." *(2 Clement 5:2–4)*

What is little and what is big

126

For the master says in the gospel, "If you have not kept what is little, who will give you what is big? For I say to you, one who is faithful in what is least is also faithful in what is great." *(2 Clement 8:5)*

The two will be one

127

For when the master himself was asked by someone when his kingdom would come, he said, "When the two will be one, and the outer like the inner, and the male with the female neither male nor female." Now the two are one when we speak truth to each other and there is one soul in two bodies with no hypocrisy. And by the inside like the outside he means this: he means that the inside is the soul and he means that the outside is the body. Therefore, just as your body is visible, so also let your soul be evident in good works. And by "the male with the female neither male nor female" he means this, that when a brother sees a sister he should not think of her at all as female, nor should she think of him at all as male. When you do these things, he says, my father's kingdom will come. *(2 Clement 12:2–6)*

Compare Gospel of Thomas saying 22: "Jesus saw some babies nursing. He said to his followers, 'These nursing babies are like those who enter the kingdom.' They said to him, 'Then shall we enter the kingdom as babies?' Jesus said to them, 'When you make the two into one, and when you make the inner like the outer and the outer like the inner, and the upper like the lower, and when you make male and female into a single one, so that the male will not be male nor the female be female, when you make eyes in place of an eye, a hand in place of a hand, a foot in place of a foot, an image in place of an image, then you will enter [the kingdom]."

THE RIGHT LIKE THE LEFT

Concerning this the master says in a mystery, "If you do not make what is on the right like what is on the left and what is on the left like what is on the right, and what is above like what is below, and what is behind like what is before, you will not recognize the kingdom." *(Martyrdom of Peter 9)*

THOSE WHO ARE WITH ME

129

Indeed, I (Marcellus) heard that he also said, "Those who are with me have not understood me." *(Acts of Peter 10)*

ONE WHO RANSOMS SOULS
FROM IDOLS

130

For thus we were taught by the savior, who said, "Whoever ransoms souls from idols will be great in my kingdom." *(Acts of Thomas 6)*

ENTER GOD'S KINGDOM THROUGH TRIBULATIONS

131

And again he said to us, "You must enter God's kingdom through many tribulations." *(Prochorus, Acts of John)*

I AM THE HOPE OF THE HOPELESS

132

"I am the hope of the hopeless, the helper of those with no helper, the treasure of the needy, the doctor of the sick, the resurrection of the dead." *(Epistle of the Apostles 21)*

Are the fingers alike?

133

And we said to him, "O master, do we have one hope of the inheritance together with them?"

He answered and said to us, "Are the fingers of the hand alike or the heads of grain in the field? Or do the fruit-bearing trees give the same fruit? Do they not produce fruit according to their nature?"

And we said to him, "O master, are you speaking to us once again in parables?"

And he said to us, "Do not be grieved. In truth I say to you, you are my brothers, companions in heaven's kingdom with my father, for so it has pleased him. In truth I say to you, I shall also give this hope to those whom you will have taught and who have become believers in me." *(Epistle of the Apostles 32)*

WINE FROM THORNS

134

And Jesus said, "Who can produce wine from thorns or wheat from thistles?" *(Dialogue Between Christ and the Devil 5)*

WHOEVER HEARS ME

135

"For whoever hears me and does what I say hears the one who sent me." *(Justin, Apology 1.16.10)*

Divisions and factions

136

"There will be divisions and factions." *(Justin, Dialogue with Trypho 35.3)*

In whatever circumstances i find you

137

Therefore our master Jesus Christ also said, "In whatever circumstances I find you, in them shall I also judge you." *(Justin, Dialogue with Trypho 47.5)*

You are whitewashed tombs

"You are whitewashed tombs, filled inside with bones of the dead, because the person who is alive is not in you." *(Naassene Exegesis, in Hippolytus, Refutation of All Heresies 5.8.23)*

Days will come when vines will grow

As the elders who had seen John, the follower of the master, recalled that they heard from him how the master taught about these times and said, "Days will come when vines will grow, each having ten thousand branches, and on each branch ten thousand twigs, and on each twig ten thousand shoots, and on each shoot ten thousand bunches, and on each bunch ten thousand grapes, and each grape, when pressed, will yield twenty-five measures of wine. And when one of the holy ones takes a bunch, another bunch will call out, 'I am better, take me, praise the master through me.' Likewise, again: a grain of wheat will grow ten thousand heads, and each head will have ten thousand grains, and each grain will yield five portions of the finest pure flour. And the other fruit and seeds and grass will produce proportionately. And all the animals will eat of this produce of the earth and be at peace and in harmony with one another, and completely subject to people." *(Papias, in Irenaeus, Against Heresies 5.33.3)*

One Who Has Not Been Tempted

140

"No one who has not been tempted should attain the heavenly realms." *(Tertullian, On Baptism 20)*

If Two Come Together

141

"If two come together into one and they say to this mountain, 'Get up and throw yourself into the sea,' it will happen." (*Didascalia 3.7.2*)

BLESSINGS ON THOSE WHO
ARE PERSECUTED

142

"Blessings on those who are persecuted for my sake, for they will have a place where they will not be persecuted." *(Clement of Alexandria, Miscellanies 4.6.41)*

———————

Compare Gospel of Thomas saying 68: "Jesus said, 'Blessings on you when you are hated and persecuted, and no place will be found, wherever you have been persecuted.'"

My mystery is for me

"My mystery is for me and the sons of my house."
(Clement of Alexandria, Miscellanies 5.10.63)

Compare Gospel of Thomas saying 62: "Jesus said, 'I disclose my mysteries to those [who are worthy] of [my] mysteries. Do not let your left hand know what your right hand is doing.'"

Parable of the Wise Fisherman

144

For now I say nothing about the parable in the gospel, which says, "Heaven's kingdom is like a person who has cast a dragnet into the sea and makes a selection of the better ones from the multitude of fish that were caught." *(Clement of Alexandria, Miscellanies 6.11.95)*

My love I give

145

"My love to you I give." *(Clement of Alexandria, Who Is the Rich Person Who Will Be Saved? 37.4)*

SAVE YOURSELF

Therefore the savior says, "Save yourself, you and your soul (or life)." *(Theodotus, in Clement of Alexandria, Excerpts from Theodotus 2.2)*

BECAUSE OF THE WEAK I WAS WEAK

And then Jesus says, "Because of the weak I was weak, and because of the hungry I was hungry, and because of the thirsty I was thirsty." *(Origen, Commentary on Matthew 13.2)*

EXPERT MONEY CHANGERS

"Be expert money changers." *(Origen, Commentary on John 19.7.2)*

ASK FOR BIG THINGS

149

"Ask for big things, and little things will be given to you as well. Ask for heavenly things, and earthly things will be given to you as well." *(Origen, Selections on Psalms 4.4)*

Whoever is near me

"Whoever is near me is near the fire; whoever is far from me is far from the kingdom." *(Origen, Homilies on Jeremiah 3.3)*

Complete the work of humankind

"[Turn back], and each one [of you bring to completion the] work of humankind, [and each] one of you [show] your devotion to [this assurance] of your [own] new [birth (?)]. Come . . . , and [join] the angels in heaven." *(Berlin 20915, D-13 [↓] 7–14)*

THE LORD'S PRAYER:
MAY YOUR HOLY SPIRIT COME

152

For in that gospel, instead of "May your kingdom come," it says this: "May your holy spirit come upon us and cleanse us." *(Gregory of Nyssa, On the Lord's Prayer 3)*

MY POWER, POWER

153

And the master called out and said, "My power, power, you have abandoned me." And when he said this, he was taken up. *(Gospel of Peter 5:5)*

That one whom you see laughing

154

The savior said to me, "That one whom you see upon the cross, glad and laughing, is the living Jesus. But that one into whose hands and feet they hammer the nails is the fleshy part, which is the substitute that is being put to shame, the one who came into being in his likeness. But look at him and me." *(Nag Hammadi Apocalypse of Peter 81, 14–24)*

The gate of life

155

Therefore, since he himself is a true prophet, he said, "I am the gate of life; one who enters through me enters into life." *(Pseudo-Clementine Homilies 3.52)*

Good and bad things come

156

The prophet of truth said, "Good things must come," he says, "and blessings on one through whom they come. Similarly, bad things must come, but alas for one through whom they come." *(Pseudo-Clementine Homilies 12.29)*

You see me in yourselves

157

"Thus you see me in yourselves, as one of you sees yourself in water or in a mirror." *(Pseudo-Cyprian, On Mounts Sinai and Zion 13)*

THE DAY

"I am the day." *(Eusebius, Against Marcellus 1.2)*

I AM YOU

And he spoke to me and said, "I am you and you are I, and wherever you are, I am there, and in all things am I sown. And from wherever you wish, you gather me, and when you gather me, you gather yourself." *(Gospel of Eve, in Epiphanius, Panarion 26.3.1)*

I am knocking

160

"I am knocking, and if anyone opens for me, we shall enter for that person, I and my father, and we shall make a home with that person." *(Epiphanius, Panarion 69.63)*

That person is i

161

"So now again, in truth I say to you, every person who will receive that mystery of the ineffable and complete it in all its types and all its patterns is a person who is in the world but is superior to all the angels, and will be greatly superior to all of them. . . . And in truth I say to you, that person is I and I am that person. . . . These things, then, I say to you, knowing that I shall give you the mystery of the ineffable, which is, that mystery is I and I am that mystery. So now not only will you reign with me, but all people who will receive the mystery of the ineffable will become fellow kings with me in my kingdom. And I am they and they are I. But my throne will be superior to them." *(Pistis Sophia 96)*

ONE IN A THOUSAND

162

The savior answered and said to Mary, "I say to you, there will be found one in a thousand, two in ten thousand, for the completion of the mystery of the first mystery." *(Pistis Sophia 134)*

I THROW FIRE UPON THE EARTH

163

Jesus, who is Aberamentho, said to his followers, "In truth I say to you, when I came I did not bring anything to the world except this fire and this water and this wine and this blood. I brought the water and the fire from the place of light of the lights of the treasury of light. I brought the wine and the blood from the place of Barbelo. And after a short time my father sent me the holy spirit in the form of a dove. The fire and the water and the wine have come into being to cleanse all the sins of the world. The blood, on the other hand, became for me a sign concerning the body of humankind, which I received in the place of Barbelo, the great power of the invisible God. The spirit also leads all the souls and takes them to the place of light. For this reason I said to you, 'I have come to throw fire upon the earth'—that is, I have come to cleanse the sins of the whole world with fire." *(Pistis Sophia 141)*

BLESSINGS ON ONE WHO HAS CRUCIFIED THE WORLD

164

The living Jesus answered and said to his apostles, "Blessings on one who has crucified the world and has not let the world crucify him."

The apostles answered in a single voice and said, "Master, teach us how to crucify the world, that it may not crucify us, or we would be destroyed and lose our lives."

The living Jesus answered and said, "The person who has crucified it is the person who has found my word and has completed it according to the will of the one who has sent me." *(First Book of Jeu 1)*

Your soul becomes thoughtful

165

The apostles answered and said, "Speak to us, master, that we may hear you. We have followed you with our whole heart. We have forsaken fathers, we have forsaken mothers, we have forsaken vineyards and fields, we have forsaken possessions, we have forsaken the greatness of royalty, and we have followed you, that you might teach us about the life of your father who has sent you."

The living Jesus answered and said, "This is the life of my father, that you receive your soul from the generation of the mind, and it stops being earthly and becomes thoughtful through what I say to you in the course of my speaking, so that you complete it and are saved from the ruler of this age and his traps, which are countless. But you, my followers, be eager to receive my word with assurance so that you know it, in order that the ruler of this age may not contend with you, this one who did not find any of his commandments in me, in order that you also, O my apostles, may complete my word for me, and I myself shall liberate you, and you will become whole through a freedom that is without defect. As the spirit of the advocate is whole, so also will you be whole, through the liberation of the spirit of the holy advocate." *(First Book of Jeu 2)*

BLESSINGS ON THE PERSON
WHO HAS KNOWN THESE THINGS

166

All the apostles, Matthew and John, Philip and Bartholomew and James, answered in a single voice and said, "Master Jesus, living one, whose goodness spreads over those who have found your wisdom and your form in which you have given light, light-giving light that has enlightened our hearts, until we received the light of life, word of truth that through knowledge teaches us the hidden knowledge of the master Jesus, the living one!"

The living Jesus answered and said, "Blessings on the person who has known these things. That person has brought heaven down and has lifted the earth and has sent it to heaven, and has come to the middle, for it is nothing." *(First Book of Jeu 3)*

Whoever forsakes father and mother

167

"Whoever forsakes father and mother and brother and sister and wife and child and possessions, and bears his cross, and follows me will receive the promises that I have promised him. And I shall give them the mystery of my hidden father, for they have loved what is theirs and have fled from the one who persecutes them violently."
(Untitled Gnostic Text, Bruce Codex, 15)

I HAVE SOMETHING TO SAY

168

"Remember what I said between me and you on the Mount of Olives: I have something to say, I have no one to whom to say it." *(Manichaean Psalm Book 187,27–29)*

I AM NEAR AS YOUR CLOTHES

169

He is not far from us, my brothers, as he said when he was preaching, "I am near you, like the clothes of your body." *(Manichaean Psalm Book 239,23–24)*

YOU ARE CAIN'S CHILDREN

Our redeemer said to them, "You are Cain's children and not Abraham's children." *(Aphrahat, Demonstration 16.8)*

POSSESS NOTHING

"Possess nothing on earth." *(Ephrem the Syrian, Testament)*

I AM WEARY

"How long shall I be with you and speak with you? . . . I am weary of this generation. They put me to the test ten times, but these have done so twenty times, ten times and ten times." *(Ephrem the Syrian, Commentary on the Diatessaron 17.6)*

THE WEAK WILL BE SAVED

For he said to us when he was teaching, "The weak will be saved through the strong." *(Apostolic Church Ordinances 26)*

Go into the houses of
tax collectors and whores

He says, "Everyone who does not walk in my footsteps and go into the houses of tax collectors and whores and teach them, as I have shown him, will not be perfect." *(Book of Steps 2.6.2)*

As you are found

He said, "As you are found, you will be taken up." *(Book of Steps 3.3)*

Renounce all that one has

176

"If one will not renounce all that one has and bear one's cross and follow me and imitate me, one is not worthy of me." *(Book of Steps 3.5)*

The inside and outside of the cup and dish

177

As the master says, "Blind Pharisee, wash the inside of the cup and the dish that the outside might also be clean, for the one who made the inside also made the outside." *(Symeon of Mesopotamia, Homilies 8.1 [type III])*

GOD'S KINGDOM IS SPREAD OUT
UPON THE EARTH

178

As the master says, "God's kingdom is spread out upon the earth, and people do not see it." *(Symeon of Mesopotamia, Homilies B35)*

YOU HAVE REJECTED THE
LIVING ONE

179

But, he said, when the apostles asked what ought to be thought about the Jewish prophets, who were believed to have proclaimed his coming beforehand, our master was upset that they still had such thoughts, and answered, "You have rejected the living one who is before you, and you speak idly about the dead." *(Augustine, Against the Adversary of the Law and the Prophets 2.4.14)*

THE BURIED WILL BE RAISED

180

Jesus says, "There is nothing buried that will not be raised." *(Burial shroud from Oxyrhynchus)*

From filth, to filth

181

Our rabbis taught as follows: when Rabbi Eliezer was arrested for heresy, he was brought before the court to be judged. The ruler said to him, "How can a wise person like you occupy yourself with such idle things?"

He answered, "I acknowledge that the judge is right."

The ruler thought that Eliezer was speaking of him, though he really was referring to his heavenly father. The ruler said, "Because you have acknowledged that I am right, I pardon you: you are acquitted."

When Eliezer came home, his followers came to console him, but he would accept no consolation. Rabbi Akiba said to him, "Master, will you permit me to say something from what you have taught me?"

He answered, "Say it."

"Master," Akiba said, "perhaps some teaching of the heretics had been communicated to you and you approved of it, and for that reason you were arrested."

Eliezer answered, "Akiba, you have reminded me. Once I was walking in the upper market of Sepphoris when I came across one of the followers of Jesus the Nazarene, Jacob of Kefar-Sekaniah by name, who said to me, 'It is written in your law, "You shall not bring the fee of a prostitute into the house of the Lord your God" (Deuteronomy 23:18). May such money be used to build a latrine for the high priest?' I gave no answer. Then he said to me, 'Thus was I taught by Jesus the Nazarene: "'As the fee of a prostitute has she gathered them, and to the fee of a prostitute shall they return' (Micah 1:7); from a place of filth has it come, to a place of filth shall it go."'

"This explanation pleased me very much, and that is why I was arrested for heresy, for I transgressed the scriptural words, 'Keep your way far from her'—that is, from heresy—'and do not go near the door of her house'—that is, the ruling power" (Proverbs 5:8). *(Babylonian Talmud, 'Abodah Zarah 16b–17a)*

I HAVE NOT COME TO ABOLISH
THE LAW OF MOSES

182

Imma Shalom, Rabbi Eliezer's wife, was Rabban Gamaliel's sister. A certain philosopher lived in his neighborhood, and he had the reputation of never accepting bribes. They wanted to play a trick on him, so Imma brought him a golden lamp, came before him, and said to him, "I want to be given my share of my father's estate."

The philosopher answered, "Then divide it."

But Gamaliel said to him, "This is decreed for us: where there is a son, a daughter may not inherit."

The philosopher said, "Since the day you were exiled from your land, the law of Moses has been undone and the law of the gospel has been given, in which it is written, 'A son and a daughter inherit equally.'"

The next day Gamaliel brought him a Libyan ass. The philosopher said to them, "Look at the end of the gospel, where it is written, 'I, the gospel, have not come to abolish the law of Moses, nor (or but) to add to the law of Moses. It is written in the law, where there is a son, a daughter may not inherit.' "

Imma said to him, "May your light shine like a lamp."

But Rabban Gamaliel said to him, "An ass has come and knocked over the lamp." *(Babylonian Talmud, Shabbath 116a–116b)*

WHO SET ME OVER YOU?

A person said to him, "Master, my brother (wants) to share (with me) my father's blessing."

(Jesus) said to him, "Who placed me over you (to determine your) share?" *('Abd al-Jabbār, Book on the Signs of Muhammad's Prophecy)*

Compare Gospel of Thomas saying 72: "A [person said] to him, 'Tell my brothers to divide my father's possessions with me.' He said to the person, 'Mister, who made me a divider?' He turned to his followers and said to them, 'I am not a divider, am I?' "

I HAVE COME TO ACT ACCORDING TO THE LAW

Thus, the Messiah came to revive the law and to put it into practice, and said, "I have come to act according to the law and the orders of the prophets before me. I have not come to abolish but to complete. It is easier in God's eyes for heaven to fall upon the earth than to abolish anything from the law of Moses. So if any person sets aside anything of this, that person will be called small in heaven's kingdom." (*'Abd al-Jabbār, Book on the Signs of Muhammad's Prophecy*)

I HAVE CURED THE SICK BUT NOT THE FOOL

185

Jesus said, "I have treated the person with leprosy and the blind person, and I have cured them, but when I have treated the fool, I have failed to cure him." *(al-Ibshihi, Al-Mustatraf [Novelties], 1.20)*

WHOEVER KNOWS

186

Jesus said, "Whoever knows and does and teaches will be called great in heaven's kingdom." *(al-Ghazali, Revival of the Religious Sciences, 1.8)*

Offering wisdom

Jesus said, "Do not offer wisdom to those who are not worthy of it, or you might harm it, and do not withhold it from those who are worthy of it, or you might harm them. Be like a gentle doctor who puts the medicine on the diseased spot. Whoever offers wisdom to those who are not worthy of it is a fool, and whoever withholds it from those who are worthy of it is an evildoer. Wisdom has rights and rightful owners, so give each what is appropriate." *(al-Ghazali, Revival of the Religious Sciences, 1.30)*

Evil scholars are like rocks, latrines, graves

Jesus said, "Evil scholars are like a rock that has fallen at the mouth of a brook: it does not drink the water, nor does it let the water flow to the plants. And evil scholars are like the drainpipe of a latrine that is plastered outside but filthy inside; or like graves that are decorated outside but contain dead people's bones inside." *(al-Ghazali, Revival of the Religious Sciences, 1.49)*

On the fallen rock, compare Gospel of Thomas saying 102: "Jesus said, 'Alas for the Pharisees, for they are like a dog sleeping in the cattle manger, for it does not eat or [let] the cattle eat'"; also Gospel of Thomas saying 39, and Unknown Saying 21.

ANYONE WHO HEARS
AND EXAGGERATES

189

Jesus said to the followers, "What would you do if you saw your brother sleeping and the wind had lifted up his clothes?"

They said, "We would cover him up."

He said, "No, you would expose him."

They said, "God forbid! Who would do this?"

He said, "Any one of you who hears a word concerning his brother and adds to it, and relates it with the additions." *(al-Ghazali, Revival of the Religious Sciences, 2.134)*

No one is poorer than I

When Jesus was asked, "How are you this morning?" he would answer, "Unable to anticipate what I hope for or put off what I fear, bound by my works, with all my good in someone else's hand. There is no poor person poorer than I." *(al-Ghazali, Revival of the Religious Sciences, 2.168)*

No one taught me

Jesus was asked, "Who taught you?"

He answered, "No one taught me. I saw that the ignorance of the fool was shameful, so I avoided it." *(al-Ghazali, Revival of the Religious Sciences, 3.52)*

Do Not Speak

192

Jesus was asked by some people, "Show us the way by which we may enter paradise."

He said, "Do not speak at all."

They said, "We cannot do that."

He said, "Then say only what is good." *(al-Ghazali, Revival of the Religious Sciences, 3.87)*

My Tongue Is Not Accustomed to Evil

193

Jesus passed by a pig and said to it, "Go in peace."

They said, "O spirit of God, do you speak like this to a pig?"

He answered, "I do not want my tongue to grow accustomed to evil." *(al-Ghazali, Revival of the Religious Sciences, 3.94)*

THE DEAD DOG'S TEETH ARE WHITE

194

Malik, son of Dinar, said this: one day Jesus was walking with his followers, and they passed by the carcass of a dog.

The followers said, "How this dog stinks!"

But Jesus said, "How white are its teeth!" *(al-Ghazali, Revival of the Religious Sciences, 3.108)*

God has given me no resting place

195

It is recorded that one day Jesus was greatly troubled by the rain and thunder and lightning, and he began to seek shelter. His eye fell on a tent a ways away, but when he came to it, he found a woman inside, so he turned away from it. Then he noticed a cave in a mountain, but when he came to it, there was a lion in it.

Laying his hand on the lion, he said, "My God, you have given everything a resting place, but to me have you given none."

Then God revealed to him, "Your resting place is in the house of my mercy. . . ." *(al-Ghazali, Revival of the Religious Sciences, 3.153)*

Compare Gospel of Thomas saying 86: "Jesus said, '[Foxes have] their dens and birds have their nests, but the child of humankind has no place to lay his head and rest' "; Matthew 8:20 (Q); Luke 9:58 (Q).

No one is richer than i

196

Jesus used to say, "My seasoning is hunger, my undergarment is fear of God, my outer garment is wool, my fire in winter is the sun's rays, my lamp is the moon, my riding beast is my feet, and my food and fruit are what the earth produces. At night I have nothing and in the morning I have nothing, yet there is no one on earth richer than I." *(al-Ghazali, Revival of the Religious Sciences, 3.159)*

Whoever seeks the world

197

Jesus said, "Whoever seeks the world is like one who drinks seawater. The more he drinks, the more his thirst increases, until it kills him." *(al-Ghazali, Revival of the Religious Sciences, 3.161)*

Money is like mud

The followers said to Jesus, "How is it that you can walk on water and we cannot?"

He said to them, "What do you think of the dinar and the dirham (pieces of money)?"

They answered, "They are precious."

He said, "But to me they are the same as mud."
(al-Ghazali, Revival of the Religious Sciences, 3.175)

JESUS' COMB AND JUG

199

Jesus the Messiah used to take nothing with him except for a comb and a jug. Then he saw a person combing his beard with his fingers, so he threw away the comb, and he saw another person drinking from a river with his hands, so he threw away the jug. *(al-Ghazali, Revival of the Religious Sciences, 4.182)*

THIS WORLD IS A BRIDGE

200

Jesus said, "This world is a bridge. Pass over it, but do not build your dwelling there." *(Inscription from a mosque at Fatehpur Sikri, India)*

———————

Compare Gospel of Thomas saying 42: "Jesus said, 'Be passersby.'"

Notes

1. Compare Gospel of Thomas prologue; Unknown Saying 44; Secret Book of James 2,7–16. "Thomas," from Aramaic or Syriac, means "twin."

2. Compare Gospel of Thomas saying 1; John 8:51–52.

3. Compare Gospel of Thomas saying 2; Unknown Sayings 26, 50, 56, 65; Matthew 7:7–8 (Q); Luke 11:9–10 (Q); also al-Ghazali, *Revival of the Religious Sciences*, 3.151: "He said again, 'The world seeks and is sought. If a person seeks the next world, this world seeks him until he obtains all his sustenance in it, but if a person seeks this world, the next world seeks him until death comes and takes him by the throat' " (D. S. Margoliouth, "Christ in Islam," p. 177).

4. Compare Gospel of Thomas sayings 3, 113; Unknown Sayings 45, 63, 66, 79, 178; Luke 17:20–21; Manichaean Psalm Book 160,20–21: "Heaven's kingdom, look, it is inside us, look, it is outside us. If we believe in it, we shall live in it forever"; Manichaean Psalm Book 219,20: "Blessings on one who will know one's soul (or life, self)." "Know yourself" was among the inscriptions at the Greek oracular center at Delphi, and this imperative was widely discussed in ancient literature.

5. Compare Gospel of Thomas saying 4; Unknown Saying 22; Manichaean Psalm Book 192,2–3: "To the old people with gray

147

hair the little children give instruction; those six years old give instruction to those sixty years old"; Infancy Gospel of Thomas 7:3. In general compare Matthew 11:25–27 (Q); Luke 10:21–22 (Q). On the first and the last, compare Matthew 20:16 (Q); Luke 13:30 (Q); Mark 10:31; Matthew 19:30; Barnabas 6:13. "A little child seven days old" probably indicates an uncircumcised child, since a Jewish boy was to be circumcised on the eighth day, or it could mean a child of the sabbath of the week of creation.

6. Compare Gospel of Thomas sayings 5, 6; Manichaean Kephalaia 65 163,26–29; Unknown Saying 180; Mark 4:22; Luke 8:17; Matthew 10:26 (Q); Luke 12:2 (Q).

7. Compare Gospel of Thomas sayings 5, 6, 14; in general compare Matthew 6:1–18; Didache 8:1–3. "Do not do what you hate" is the negative formulation of the golden rule.

8. Compare Gospel of Thomas saying 7. Here, as in Plato, the lion may well symbolize what is passionate and bestial in human life. A person may consume passion or be consumed by passion!

9. Compare Gospel of Thomas saying 24; Unknown Saying 61; Matthew 6:22–23 (Q); Luke 11:34–35 (Q), 36 (Q?).

10. Compare Gospel of Thomas saying 26; Matthew 7:3–5 (Q); Luke 6:41–42 (Q). A similar saying is attributed to Rabbi Tarfon in the Babylonian Talmud.

11. Compare Gospel of Thomas saying 27; Clement of Alexandria, Miscellanies 3.15.99; Tertullian, Against the Jewish People 4.2; Symeon of Mesopotamia, Homilies 35.1.

12. Compare Gospel of Thomas saying 28. In gnostic and other texts a person who is ignorant is often said to be drunk.

13. Compare Gospel of Thomas saying 29.

14. Compare Gospel of Thomas sayings 30, 77; Ephrem the Syrian, Commentary on the Diatessaron 14.24: "Where there is

one, there also am I, or someone might be sad from what is lonely, since he himself is our joy and he himself is with us. And where there are two, there also shall I be, since his mercy and grace overshadow us. And when we are three, we assemble just as in church, which is the body of Christ perfected and his image expressed"; Manichaean Psalm Book 54,19–30: "The strangers with whom I mingled do not know me. They tasted my sweetness and wished to keep me with them. I became life for them, but they became death for me. I bore them up, and they wore me as a garment upon them. I am in all, I bear the heavens, I am the foundation, I support the earths, I am the light that shines forth, that makes the souls rejoice. I am the life of the world, I am the milk that is in all trees, I am the sweet water that is under the children of matter."

15. Compare Gospel of Thomas saying 31; Mark 6:4; Matthew 13:57; Luke 4:23–24; John 4:44; on wisdom and a doctor, compare Unknown Saying 187.

16. Compare Gospel of Thomas saying 32; Matthew 5:14; 7:24–25 (Q); Luke 6:47–48 (Q).

17. Compare Gospel of Thomas saying 33; Matthew 10:27 (Q); Luke 12:3 (Q); Matthew 5:15 (Q); Luke 11:33 (Q); Mark 4:21; Luke 8:16; Clement of Alexandria, Miscellanies 6.15.124.

18. Compare Gospel of Thomas saying 36; Matthew 6:25–33 (Q), 34; Luke 12:22–31 (Q), 32. The original reading of Matthew 6:28 in Codex Sinaiticus also refers to carding wool. Al-Ghazali, *Revival of the Religious Sciences*, 4.190, has a similar saying of Jesus: "Consider the birds: they do not sow or reap or gather into barns, yet God sustains them day by day. If, however, you say, 'But we have a bigger belly than they have,' then I say to you, consider the cattle, how God has provided their sustenance for them" (from the Latin in Michael Asin, *Logia et Agrapha Domini*

Jesu, p. 409; see also Samarqandi, *Awakening of the Negligent*, p. 168, for a similar saying on the ants [English translation in James Robson, *Christ in Islam*, pp. 72–73]).

19. Compare Gospel of Thomas saying 37; Unknown Sayings 41, 75, 113; Manichaean Psalm Book 99,26–30: "The saying of Jesus the redeemer came to [me (?), as] is appropriate: The vain garment of this flesh have I stripped off, and I am saved and purified; I have caused the clean feet of my soul to trample upon it confidently; with the gods that are clothed with Christ have I stood in line."

20. Compare Gospel of Thomas saying 38; Matthew 13:17 (Q); Luke 10:24 (Q); 17:22; John 7:33–36; Unknown Sayings 95, 129, 168; Irenaeus, Against Heresies 1.20.2: "Often have I desired to hear one of these sayings, and I have had no one to tell (me)"; Acts of John 98: "John, there must be one person to hear these things from me, for I need someone who is going to hear"; Cyprian, Three Books of Testimonies to Quirinus 3.29: "For a time will come and you will seek me, both you and those who will come after, to hear a word of wisdom and understanding, and you will not find (me)."

21. Compare Gospel of Thomas saying 39; Matthew 23:13 (Q); Luke 11:52 (Q); Pseudo-Clementine Recognitions 2.30.1; Unknown Saying 188; Matthew 10:16; Ignatius, Polycarp 2:2. For comparisons to snakes and doves, see also the Midrash Rabbah, Song of Songs. On being innocent as doves, compare an Islamic saying of Jesus: "Jesus said, 'If you can be simple as doves regarding God, do so. Nothing is more simple than a dove. For you may take its two nestlings from under it and kill them, and yet later the dove will return to that very place and bring forth other nestlings there again'" (from the Latin in Asin, *Logia et Agrapha Domini Jesu*, p. 567).

22. Compare Gospel of Thomas saying 4; Unknown Saying 5 (and parallels).

23. Compare Gospel of Thomas saying 11.

24. Compare Gospel of Thomas saying 104. Also compare, in general, Mark 1:1–11; Matthew 3:1–17; Luke 3:1–22; John 1:19–34; Gospel of the Hebrews 3; Gospel of the Ebionites 1a, 1b, 3, 4.

25. Compare Gospel of the Hebrews 4b, 4c, 4d, 4e; Unknown Saying 94. On the cosmic mother, compare also Unknown Sayings 76, 84.

26. Compare Gospel of the Hebrews 6a; Unknown Saying 3 (and parallels).

27. Compare Gospel of the Hebrews 8: "In the Gospel according to the Hebrews, which the Nazarenes are used to reading, this is regarded as among the worst offenses: 'one who has brought distress to his brother's spirit.'"

28. On James the Righteous, the brother of Jesus, compare Gospel of Thomas saying 12; 1 Corinthians 15:7; Hegesippus's Memoirs, in Eusebius, Church History 2.23.4–7; several tractates from the Nag Hammadi library, including the Secret Book of James. Here and in other sayings the translation "child of humankind" reproduces the phrase traditionally translated "son of man."

29. In general compare Mark 1:16–20; Matthew 4:18–22; Luke 5:1–11; John 1:35–42, 43–51; Gospel of Peter 14:1–3. The Gospel of the Ebionites mentions twelve apostles but lists only eight names.

30. Compare Mark 3:31–35; Matthew 12:46–50; Luke 8:19–21; Gospel of Thomas saying 99; 2 Clement 9:11. For another perspective on Jesus' father and mother, compare an Islamic saying of Jesus: "This is the meaning of the saying of the Messiah, son

of Mary, when he had water in his right hand and bread in his left: 'This is my father, this is my mother.' Thus he considered water his father and he considered food his mother, because water relates to the earth as semen relates to a woman. The earth brings forth from water as a woman conceives from semen" (from the Latin in Asin, *Logia et Agrapha Domini Jesu*, p. 568). On this Islamic saying, compare Unknown Sayings 25, 51 (and parallels).

31. In general compare Matthew 9:13 and 12:7, citing Hosea 6:6.

32. In general compare Mark 14:12; Matthew 26:17; Luke 22:8–9, 15. Here in the Gospel of the Ebionites Jesus is made to recommend a vegetarian diet. Compare also Gospel of the Ebionites 3, on John the Baptizer eating only wild honey that was like a pancake (Greek *egkris*), and not locusts (Greek *akris*). For similar descriptions of Jesus as a vegetarian, compare Unknown Saying 196 (and parallels).

33. Compare Matthew 6:9–13 (Q); Luke 11:2–4 (Q). On the origin of one's bread, compare also the Islamic saying of Jesus in which Jesus responds to a person asking for advice by saying, "Consider your bread, where it comes from" (from the Latin in Asin, *Logia et Agrapha Domini Jesu*, p. 593). For another alternate reading of the Lord's Prayer, see Unknown Saying 152.

34. Compare Matthew 18:21–22 (Q); Luke 17:4 (Q).

35. Compare Mark 10:17–25; Matthew 19:16–24; Luke 18:18–25; Unknown Sayings 103, 118, 119; al-Ghazali, *Revival of the Religious Sciences*, 1.177: "Jesus said, 'If a person sends a beggar away empty from his house, the angels will not visit that house for seven nights'" (Margoliouth, "Christ in Islam," p. 59).

36. Compare Matthew 24:45–51; 25:14–30.

37. This quotation from the Gospel of the Nazoreans is given in the context of a discussion of Matthew 10:34–36 ([Q]; compare

Luke 12: 51–53 [Q]; Gospel of Thomas saying 16). The phrase "the ones whom my heavenly father has given me" sounds Johannine.

38. Compare 2 Clement 4:5; in general, Matthew 7:23 (Q); Luke 13:27 (Q); Psalm 6:8. This passage is said to derive from the *Ioudaikon*, the "Jewish (gospel)."

39. Compare Gospel of the Egyptians 1b, 1c; Unknown Sayings 72, 77; in general compare Unknown Sayings 40, 42.

40. In general compare Unknown Saying 39 (and parallels).

41. Compare Unknown Sayings 19, 127 (and parallels).

42. In general compare Unknown Saying 39 (and parallels).

43. Compare Unknown Saying 125 (and parallels).

44. Compare Unknown Saying 1 (and parallels). On Matthew, or Matthaios, as one who, according to Papias, compiled a collection of sayings of Jesus, see the introduction.

45. In general compare Unknown Saying 4 (and parallels). Judas the twin as Jesus' "true friend" calls to mind the beloved disciple in John and perhaps also in the Secret Gospel of Mark; compare Unknown Saying 86 on Mary of Magdala as a beloved disciple.

46. This contrast between the visible, physical world and the invisible, spiritual world is also made elsewhere—for instance, in Plato's Phaedo. On being students or apprentices, compare Unknown Saying 47 ("you are children").

47. On being immature children, compare 1 Corinthians 3:1–3; Ephesians 4:13–14; Hebrews 5:12–14.

48. In general compare John 1:9; 8:12; 12:46.

49. These wisdom reflections are similar to observations in Proverbs and other wisdom literature. On the wise person being like a tree by a stream, compare Psalm 1:3.

50. Compare Unknown Saying 3 (and parallels).

51. This story of plant life is vaguely like the parable of the sower (Mark 4:2–9; Matthew 13:3–9; Luke 8:4–8; Gospel of Thomas saying 9), and it is also reminiscent of the story of the life cycle of the Grain Mother and her daughter Kore as celebrated in the Eleusinian Mysteries. In the Book of Thomas, the story, with its allegorical features, also describes human reproduction and life. On sowing and reproducing bringing death, compare Unknown Sayings 39, 40, 42.

52. This description of the dire fate of people condemned to Tartaros, or hell, illustrates features typical of other descriptions of the underworld in Hesiod, Plato, the Ethiopic Apocalypse of Peter, and Dante's "Inferno." Tartarouchos is the one who controls Tartaros. For additional sayings of Jesus concerning the day of judgment, see William D. Stroker, *Extracanonical Sayings of Jesus*, pp. 61–114, especially pp. 64–71.

53. Here and in Unknown Saying 55 Jesus utters a series of twelve woes. "The prison that will perish" recalls the body as the prison of the soul in Platonic and Orphic thought, and the prisoners "bound in caves" recall the allegory of the cave in Plato's Republic.

54. In general compare Matthew 15:13; John 15:5–6; Gospel of Thomas saying 40; Isaiah 5:1–7; Matthew 13:24–30; Gospel of Thomas saying 57.

55. On the series of woes, compare Unknown Saying 53. On the blessings, compare Matthew 5:10, 11 (Q); Luke 6:22 (Q); Matthew 5:4 (Q); Luke 6:21 (Q); Gospel of Thomas sayings 68, 69; Unknown Saying 142.

56. Compare Unknown Saying 3 (and parallels).

57. On rest, compare Unknown Saying 3 (and parallels).

58. On the bridge or passage to cross, compare Unknown Saying 200. On those "chosen and alone," compare Gospel of Thomas saying 49.

59. These sayings are presented as prayers of Jesus. Besides the Lord's Prayer, compare also the first of the two prayers in the Letter of Peter to Philip 133,21–134,1: "Father, father, father of the light, who possesses the incorruptions, hear us just as [you] have taken pleasure in your holy child Jesus Christ. For he became for us an illuminator in the darkness. Yea, hear us!"

60. On truth, compare Unknown Saying 97; in general compare Unknown Sayings 3, 7.

61. Compare Unknown Saying 9 (and parallels); Matthew 15:14 (Q); Luke 6:39 (Q); Gospel of Thomas saying 34; Samarqandi, *Awakening of the Negligent*, p. 156: "What good is it for a blind person if he carries a lamp to give light to others? What good is it for a dark house if a lamp is put on its roof? What good is it for you if you speak wisely but do not act wisely?" (from the Latin in Asin, *Logia et Agrapha Domini Jesu*, p. 562).

62. In general compare Unknown Sayings 3, 6, 7 (and parallels).

63. Compare Unknown Sayings 3, 4 (and parallels).

64. In general compare Unknown Saying 146.

65. On renouncing power, compare Gospel of Thomas sayings 81, 110. On seeking and finding, compare Unknown Saying 3 (and parallels).

66. On knowing oneself, compare Unknown Sayings 4, 45.

67. On not knowing perfection, compare Unknown Sayings 45, 46, 47.

68. In general compare Gospel of Thomas sayings 18, 49.

69. Compare Unknown Saying 19 (and parallels). On entering the wedding chamber, compare Gospel of Thomas saying 75. The image of the wedding chamber as a place of unification and life is common in early Christian literature.

70. In gnostic and other texts, fullness characterizes the reign of the divine, which is full of light, and deficiency characterizes this world below, which lacks the light of the divine.

71. Compare Gospel of Thomas saying 17; 1 Corinthians 2:9; Manichaean Turfan fragment M 789; Isaiah 64:4; and others. This saying occurs frequently in Jewish and Christian literature, and a variant of it is also to be found in Plutarch, How the Young Person Should Study Poetry.

72. Compare Unknown Saying 39 (and parallels).

73. Compare Unknown Sayings 65, 198; Gospel of Thomas sayings 81, 110.

74. On love and the ethic of Jesus, compare Unknown Saying 119 (and parallels).

75. Compare Unknown Saying 19 (and parallels).

76. On the mustard seed, compare Mark 4:30–32; Matthew 13:31–32 (Q); Luke 13:18–19 (Q); Gospel of Thomas saying 20; Matthew 17:20 (Q); Luke 17:6 (Q). On the mother, compare Unknown Saying 25 (and parallels).

77. Compare Unknown Saying 39 (and parallels).

78. On being confident, compare in general Luke 24:36–39; John 14:27. "Whoever has ears to hear should hear"—a statement calling on the hearer or reader to pay close attention to the real meaning and interpretation of the saying—occurs throughout early Christian literature.

79. "Peace be with you" is a common Semitic greeting. On the child of humankind within, compare Unknown Saying 4 (and parallels).

80. On preaching the good news, compare Mark 13:10; 16:15; Matthew 4:23; 9:35; 24:14. On making followers and laying down rules, compare Matthew 28:19–20.

81. On Jesus loving Mary, compare Unknown Saying 86. On the saying about where the mind is, compare Matthew 6:21 (Q); Luke 12:34 (Q). Justin (Apology) and Clement of Alexandria (Miscellanies and Who Is the Rich Person Who Will Be Saved?) also have versions of this saying, as do Manichaean and other sources.

82. This enigmatic saying seems to recommend that all be brought to God and nothing be taken from God.

83. This may actually be a saying of Philip. The images being united with the angels may designate earthly people being united with their heavenly alter egos; sometimes this is described as the female below, like the human soul (Psyche), being united with the male above, perhaps in the wedding chamber. Compare also Unknown Saying 127 (and parallels).

84. On the mother, compare Unknown Saying 25 (and parallels).

85. On Jesus in a dyehouse, compare also the Arabic Infancy Gospel and the Paris Manuscript of the Infancy Gospel of Thomas (in Wilhelm Schneemelcher, editor, *New Testament Apocrypha*, 1.453), as well as a story from the Muslim author Tha'labi (in Robson, *Christ in Islam*, pp. 33–34). Seventy-two (or seventy) is a traditional number in Judaism and Christianity, used to specify the number of nations in the world, according to the interpretation of the rabbis.

86. On Jesus loving Mary, compare Unknown Saying 81; also Pistis Sophia 17: "You (Mary) are the one whose heart is turned toward heaven's kingdom more than all of your brothers." On the blind person and the one who can see, compare in general Matthew 15:14 (Q); Luke 6:39 (Q); Gospel of Thomas saying 34.

87. Compare Gospel of Thomas saying 19; also Lactantius, Divine Institutes 4.8; Irenaeus, Proof of the Apostolic Preaching 43; perhaps John 8:58.

88. Compare Unknown Saying 127 (and parallels).

89. On laughter, compare Unknown Saying 154.

90. On Jesus returning, compare John 7:33; 13:36; 14:3–5; 16:5, 16–20, 28. In general, on returning to one's place of origin, compare Gospel of Thomas sayings 18, 49. The number of days (550) for Jesus to linger after the resurrection compares well with the eighteen months (540 days) or 545 days mentioned elsewhere in gnostic texts, but it goes well beyond the conservative figure of forty days in Luke and Acts. On fullness, or being filled, a prominent theme in the Secret Book of James, compare Unknown Saying 70 (and the note).

91. Compare Unknown Saying 109; John 20:29.

92. Here the spirit is valued more highly than the soul, or human reason.

93. On forsaking all, compare Unknown Sayings 165, 167, 176; Mark 10:28–30; Matthew 19:27–29; Luke 18:28–30; also Matthew 10:37–38 (Q); Luke 14:26–27 (Q); Gospel of Thomas saying 55. A version of this saying about forsaking all is also found in the Manichaean Psalm Book. On not being tempted, compare the Lord's Prayer (cited at Unknown Saying 33). On being persecuted, compare Unknown Sayings 55, 94, 102, 142. On being equal to Jesus, compare Unknown Sayings 94, 96, 107, 157, 159,

160, 161. On the days in one's life, compare also an Islamic saying of Jesus: "Jesus, son of Mary, said, 'Life in this world consists of three days: yesterday, which is already past and of which you hold nothing in your hand; tomorrow, about which you do not know whether you will ever reach it or not; and today, in which you live. So take advantage of this day' " (from the Latin in Asin, *Logia et Agrapha Domini Jesu*, p. 574).

94. On seeking and finding (in this case, death), compare Unknown Saying 3 (and parallels). "<God's> kingdom" is read by emending the Coptic text from *mou* to *noute*. If the translation is understood as "put themselves to death," this saying may refer to voluntary martyrdom. On becoming better than Jesus, compare Unknown Saying 93 (and parallels). On the holy spirit as mother, compare Unknown Saying 25 (and parallels).

95. On John the Baptizer's head, compare Mark 6:14–29; Matthew 14:1–12. On prophecy until John, compare Matthew 11:12–13 (Q); Luke 16:16 (Q). On parables, compare Mark 4:10–13, 33–34; Matthew 13:10–17, 34–35; Luke 8:9–10; John 10:6; 16:25.

96. On outdoing Jesus, compare Unknown Saying 93 (and parallels).

97. On truth, compare Unknown Saying 60.

98. The translation of the parable of the date palm shoot, a parable known only from the Secret Book of James, remains somewhat tentative.

99. On faith, love, and works, compare (and contrast) Paul's enumeration of faith, hope, and love in 1 Corinthians 13:13. On the parable of the grain of wheat, compare the parable of the head of grain (Unknown Saying 108) and the parable of the sower (Mark 4:2–9; Matthew 13:3–9; Luke 8:4–8; Gospel of

Thomas saying 9), particularly the allegorical interpretation added in the synoptic gospels (Mark 4:13–20; Matthew 13:18–23; Luke 8:11–15); also al-Ghazali, *Revival of the Religious Sciences*, 3.261: "The Messiah said, 'A seed grows in the field, but it does not grow on rock. Even so, wisdom works in the heart of the humble, but it does not work in the heart of the proud. Do you not see that if a person lifts his head to the roof, it hurts him, but if he bows down his head, the roof shelters him?'" (Margoliouth, "Christ in Islam," p. 504).

100. On following Jesus, compare Unknown Sayings 105, 165, 167, 174, 176. On Jesus coming down to dwell, compare John 1:9–14; 14:23. On the roofs, see the saying of Jesus in al-Ghazali in the note to Unknown Saying 99.

101. In general compare Matthew 11:27 (Q); Luke 10:22 (Q); John 5:19–20.

102. On the word and life, compare Unknown Saying 99. On persecution, compare Unknown Sayings 55, 93, 94, 142.

103. In general compare the opening of Unknown Saying 106. On the construction "it is easier . . . than for you . . . ," compare Unknown Saying 35; Mark 10:25: "It is easier for a camel (or a rope, according to a variant reading) to go through a needle's eye than for a rich person to enter God's kingdom" (also Matthew 19:24; Luke 18:25).

104. Compare Unknown Saying 20 (and parallels).

105. On following Jesus, compare Unknown Saying 100 (and parallels). On Jesus coming and going, compare Unknown Sayings 90, 100, 104, 113.

106. On the opening of the saying, compare Unknown Saying 103.

107. This saying, in its context in the Secret Book of James, assumes that a person is composed of body, soul, and spirit (compare Unknown Saying 92). On "a fourth one in heaven," perhaps compare Unknown Saying 93 (and parallels).

108. Compare the parable of the grain of wheat (Unknown Saying 99) and the parable of the sower (Mark 4:2–9; Matthew 13:3–9; Luke 8:4–8; Gospel of Thomas saying 9). As in the synoptic gospels, an allegorical interpretation is added in the Secret Book of James.

109. Compare Unknown Saying 91; John 20:29.

110. On building a house, compare Matthew 7:24–27 (Q); Luke 6:47–49 (Q); al-Ghazali, *Revival of the Religious Sciences*, 3.153: "Jesus said, 'Who is it who builds upon the waves of the sea? That is what the world is like. Do not make it your resting place'" (Margoliouth, "Christ in Islam," p. 178). On the woe, compare Unknown Saying 104.

111. On Jesus being under a curse, compare Galatians 3:13; Deuteronomy 21:23.

112. Compare John 6:37.

113. Compare Unknown Saying 19 (and parallels).

114. Compare Mark 9:49; Leviticus 2:13. In this part of the book I do not include, among the alternate readings in New Testament gospel manuscripts, the story of the woman caught committing adultery, with its well-known saying of Jesus, "Whoever is sinless among you should be first to throw a stone at her," because it is found in a substantial number of ancient manuscripts and is incorporated into many modern versions of the New Testament as John 7:53–8:11.

115. Compare Matthew 23:12 (Q); Luke 14:7–10, 11 (Q), 12–14; 18:14 (Q).

116. Compare Mark 2:23–3:6; Matthew 12:1–14; Luke 6:1–11. On the sabbath, compare also Unknown Saying 11.

117. Compare Luke 19:10; Matthew 18:11 (in Codex Bezae and other manuscripts).

118. Compare Polycarp, *Philippians* 2:3; Clement of Alexandria, *Miscellanies* 2.18.91; passages especially from the sermon of Jesus in Matthew 5–7 and in Luke 6 (and in Q), as well as the Gospel of Thomas.

119. Compare especially the sermon of Jesus in Matthew 5–7, Luke 6, and Q; also Shepherd of Hermas, Mandates 2:4–7, and, in general, the Gospel of Thomas. On turning the other cheek and going the second mile, compare sayings from the *Toledot Yeshu* (in Günter Schlichting, *Ein jüdisches Leben Jesu*, pp. 170–71 [Hebrew text and German translation]) and al-Ghazali, *Revival of the Religious Sciences* (in Asin, *Logia et Agrapha Domini Jesu*, p. 394, English translation in Robson, *Christ in Islam*, pp. 47–48). On giving to the needy, compare Unknown Saying 35 (and parallels) and the saying of Jesus in a Turkish Manichaean text: "And with your whole heart believe this: the reward for (a piece of) bread and a cup of water (given as alms) will never vanish, but is sure" (Hans-Joachim Klimkeit, *Gnosis on the Silk Road*, p. 326).

120. Compare Matthew 5:44 (Q); Luke 6:27–28 (Q); Mark 9:40; Luke 9:50; Matthew 12:30 (Q); Luke 11:23 (Q).

121. Compare John 5:30–47; 9:29; contrast Unknown Saying 179.

122. Compare Mark 12:13–17; Matthew 22:15–22; Luke 20:20–26; Gospel of Thomas saying 100; Matthew 7:21 (Q); Luke 6:46 (Q); Mark 7:6–8 and Matthew 15:7–9 (citing Isaiah 29:13).

123. On cleanliness, compare Unknown Sayings 7, 174, 177, 181, 188. On dogs and pigs, compare Matthew 7:6; Gospel of Thomas

saying 93; Unknown Sayings 193, 194; al-Ghazali, *Revival of the Religious Sciences*, 1.43: "Jesus said, 'Do not place pearls on the necks of pigs, for wisdom is better than a pearl, and whoever scorns it is worse than pigs'" (from the Latin in Asin, *Logia et Agrapha Domini Jesu*, p. 350). On the saying in general, compare another Islamic saying of Jesus on cleanliness and purity (translated in Robson, *Christ in Islam*, pp. 52–54).

124. Compare Matthew 7:21 (Q); Luke 6:46 (Q); Unknown Saying 122.

125. Compare Matthew 10:16 (Q), 28 (Q); Luke 10:3 (Q); 12:4–5 (Q); Unknown Saying 43.

126. Compare Irenaeus, Against Heresies 2.34.3; Matthew 25:21 (Q), 23 (Q); Luke 16:10–12; 19:17 (Q). On the contrast between big and little, compare also Unknown Saying 149.

127. Compare Gospel of Thomas saying 22; Unknown Sayings 41, 88, 128, 141 (two into one); Acts of Philip 140: "For the master said to me (Philip), 'If you do not make what is below into what is above and what is on the left into what is on the right, you will not enter my kingdom'"; Manichaean Psalm Book 155,32–39: "My God, you are a marvel to tell. You are inside, you are outside, you are above, you are below, (you) who are near and are far, who are hidden and are revealed, who are silent and also speak. Yours is all the glory."

128. Compare Unknown Saying 127 (and parallels).

129. Compare Mark 8:17; Luke 18:34; John 14:9; Unknown Saying 20 (and parallels).

130. On being great in the kingdom, compare Unknown Saying 186. On the version of the Acts of Thomas cited here, see Ropes, "Agrapha," p. 348.

131. Compare Acts 14:22; Barnabas 7:11; Unknown Sayings 93, 94.

132. Compare Matthew 11:4–5 (Q); Luke 4:18; 7:22 (Q); John 11:25–26. The aretalogical form ("I am . . .") is typical of the Gospel of John and similar sources.

133. Compare Matthew 7:16–20 (Q); 12:33–35 (Q); Luke 6:43–45 (Q); Gospel of Thomas saying 45; al-Ghazali, *Revival of the Religious Sciences*, 1.26: "Jesus said, 'There are many trees, but not all of them bear fruit. There are many fruits, but not all of them are good to eat. There are many sorts of knowledge, but not all of them are useful'" (Margoliouth, "Christ in Islam," p. 59); also Manichaean Kephalaia 6 30,17–24: "Once again the illuminator said to his followers, 'There are five storehouses that have come into being since the beginning in the land of darkness. [The] five elements have come forth from them; also, from the five elements the five trees have been formed; again, from the five trees the five kinds of creatures have been formed in each of the worlds, male and female. Now the five worlds themselves have five kings, five spirits, [five] bodies, five [tastes] in each of the worlds, and they are not like [one another]'" (compare Gospel of Thomas saying 19). On parables, compare, for example, Unknown Saying 95 (and parallels). On those who will be taught and will believe, compare Unknown Sayings 105, 113.

134. Compare Unknown Saying 133 (and parallels).

135. Compare Matthew 10:40 (Q); Luke 10:16 (Q); John 5:23; 12:44–45; 13:20.

136. Didymus the Blind, On the Trinity 3.22, has a very similar version of this saying: "There will be factions and divisions among you." Compare also Mark 13:12–13; Matthew 10:21–22; 24:9–13; Luke 21:16–19; Matthew 10:34–36 (Q); Luke 12:49 (Q?), 50, 51–53 (Q); Gospel of Thomas sayings 10, 16; Unknown Saying 163; 1 Corinthians 11:18–19.

137. A similar sort of statement is to be found in Ezekiel 7:8; 18:30; 33:20. Compare Unknown Saying 175.

138. Compare Matthew 23:27 (Q); Luke 11:44 (Q); Unknown Saying 188.

139. For a comparable version of the fantastic growth of plants, see Apocalypse of Paul 22 (in Wilhelm Schneemelcher, editor, *New Testament Apocrypha*, 2.726).

140. Compare Unknown Saying 93; Mark 14:38; Matthew 26:41; Luke 22:46; Matthew 6:13 (Q); Luke 11:4 (Q) (cited at Unknown Saying 33).

141. Compare Gospel of Thomas sayings 48, 106; Matthew 18:19; 17:20 (Q); Luke 17:6 (Q); Mark 11:23; Matthew 21:21. On two becoming one (or agreeing), compare Unknown Saying 127 (and parallels). On mountains being moved, compare 1 Corinthians 13:2.

142. Compare Gospel of Thomas sayings 68, 69; Matthew 5:10, 11 (Q); Luke 6:22 (Q); Unknown Saying 93 (and parallels).

143. Compare Gospel of Thomas saying 62; Pseudo-Clementine Homilies 19.20.1; Mark 4:11; Matthew 13:11; Luke 8:10; Unknown Saying 187.

144. Compare Gospel of Thomas saying 8; Matthew 13:47–50; in Matthew 13:49–50 an allegorical interpretation is added. Such parables about fishing are also found in other Christian authors like Philoxenos of Mabbug, and a similar story is to be noted among Aesop's fables (Babrius, Fable 4).

145. Compare John 13:34; 14:27; Unknown Sayings 74, 119.

146. In general compare Unknown Saying 64; Matthew 10:39; Luke 17:33; Mark 8:35; Matthew 16:25; Luke 9:24; John 12:25.

147. In general compare Matthew 8:17; 25:35–36; 1 Corinthians 9:22; Unknown Saying 173.

148. Compare Clement of Alexandria, Miscellanies 1:28.177: "Be expert money changers, rejecting some things but keeping what is good"; 1 Thessalonians 5:21–22.

149. Compare Clement of Alexandria, Miscellanies 1.24.158; Matthew 6:33 (Q); Luke 12:31 (Q); Unknown Saying 126.

150. Compare Gospel of Thomas saying 82. This saying is also cited in Didymus the Blind, Pseudo-Ephrem, and Berlin 22220; in the last two texts the saying concludes with the phrase "far from life." Berlin 22220 has Jesus specifically identify himself as the blazing fire, and he announces that whoever is near him will burn. Compare Ignatius, Smyrnaeans 4:2, and Greek proverbs on being near or far from Zeus and the thunderbolt.

151. The attribution of this saying to Jesus remains somewhat uncertain. On the general wording of the saying, compare Hebrews 6:11–12. The theme of a new birth or of rebirth is found in the New Testament Gospel of John; compare Unknown Saying 87 (and parallels), as well as sayings of Jesus in Islamic sources. This theme is also well known in the texts of the mystery religions, where the initiate is sometimes said to be born again. On joining the angels, compare Unknown Saying 83.

152. Compare Matthew 6:10 (Q); Luke 11:2 (Q) (cited at Unknown Saying 33). This petition is also found as a variant reading to Luke 11:2 in Codex 700. For another alternate reading of the Lord's Prayer, see Unknown Saying 33.

153. On this saying of Jesus from the cross, compare Mark 15:34; Matthew 27:46; Psalm 22:1 (all read, "My God, my God, why have you abandoned me?").

154. On laughter, compare Unknown Saying 89. On the laughing Jesus, compare Second Treatise of the Great Seth 54,14–56,20. On Jesus only appearing to die on the cross, compare Qur'an, sura 4.

155. Compare the Naassene Exegesis, in Hippolytus, Refutation of All Heresies 5.8.20: "I am the true gate"; John 10:7, 9. The "I am . . ." form is typical of the Gospel of John and similar sources.

156. Compare Manichaean Psalm Book 239,27–28; Matthew 18:7 (Q); Luke 17:1 (Q).

157. Compare Eugnostos the Blessed III 75,1–5; Sophia of Jesus Christ III 98,25–99,3; Unknown Sayings 93 (and parallels, on being like Jesus), 159, 160, 161; Gospel of Thomas saying 108.

158. Compare John 8:12; 9:5; 12:46; Gospel of Thomas saying 77; Manichaean Psalm Book 54,19–30 (see the note to Unknown Saying 14). According to Eusebius, Marcellus thought Jesus identified himself as the morning star.

159. Compare Unknown Saying 157 (and parallels). Here the identity of the speaker is somewhat uncertain.

160. Compare Unknown Sayings 100, 157 (and parallels); John 14:23; Revelation 3:20.

161. Compare Unknown Saying 157 (and parallels).

162. Compare Gospel of Thomas saying 23. Variations of this saying are also known from Jewish, Christian, and Mandaean sources.

163. Compare Gospel of Thomas sayings 10, 16; Luke 12:49 (Q?); Unknown Saying 150. Barbelo is the name of the divine mother in some gnostic texts.

164. Compare Galatians 6:14; Unknown Sayings 93, 94 (and parallels).

165. On forsaking all, compare Unknown Saying 93 (and parallels). On receiving the word of Jesus, compare Unknown Sayings 1, 2 (and parallels).

166. In general, perhaps compare Unknown Saying 4 (and parallels). On what is above and below, perhaps compare Unknown Saying 127 (and parallels).

167. Compare Unknown Saying 93 (and parallels).

168. Compare Unknown Saying 20 (and parallels).

169. Compare Jeremiah 13:11. The claim that the divine is nearer than the clothes on a person's body is made by Origen, Clement of Alexandria, and Pseudo-Ezekiel; see Stroker, *Extracanonical Sayings of Jesus*, pp. 170–71.

170. In general compare Matthew 3:9 (Q); Luke 3:8 (Q); John 8:33–44.

171. Compare Matthew 6:19–20 (Q); Luke 12:33 (Q); Gospel of Thomas saying 76.

172. Compare Mark 9:19; Matthew 17:17; Luke 9:41; Numbers 14:22.

173. In general compare Unknown Sayings 147, 187.

174. On following Jesus, compare Unknown Sayings 100, 105, 165, 167, 176. On tax collectors and whores, compare Matthew 11:19 (Q); Luke 7:34 (Q); also a saying of Jesus from an Islamic source: "They (the followers) saw him coming out of a prostitute's house and said to him, 'O spirit of God, what are you doing with this kind of woman?' He answered, 'A doctor comes only to the sick'" (from the Latin in Asin, *Logia et Agrapha Domini Jesu*, p. 537).

175. Compare Unknown Saying 137 (and parallels).

176. Compare Gospel of Thomas saying 55. On renouncing all, compare Unknown Saying 93 (and parallels). On following Jesus, compare Unknown Sayings 100, 105, 165, 167, 174.

177. Compare Matthew 23:25–26 (Q); Luke 11:39–41 (Q); Gospel of Thomas saying 89.

178. Compare Gospel of Thomas saying 113; Luke 17:20–21; Unknown Saying 4 (and parallels).

179. Compare Gospel of Thomas saying 52; Acts of Thomas 170; John 5:37–40; 8:52–53; contrast Unknown Saying 121.

180. Compare Unknown Saying 6.

181. On cleanliness, compare Unknown Sayings 7, 123, 174, 177, 188.

182. Compare Unknown Sayings 183, 184; Matthew 5:17, 18 (Q), 19–20; Luke 16:17 (Q); contrast Unknown Sayings 7, 11, 31, 80, 116, 123, 174, 177.

183. Compare Gospel of Thomas saying 72; Luke 12:13–14 (Q?); Unknown Saying 182.

184. Compare Unknown Sayings 182, 186 (and parallels). On the construction "it is easier . . . than . . . ," compare Unknown Saying 103 (and the note).

185. In general compare Unknown Saying 187. Like many of the sayings of Jesus in Islamic sources, this saying presents Jesus as a teacher of wisdom; compare also the general presentation of Jesus in Q and the Gospel of Thomas, more specifically Matthew 11:19 (Q); Luke 7:35 (Q); Matthew 23:34 (Q); Luke 11:49 (Q); Gospel of Thomas sayings 1, 2, 3 (Unknown Sayings 2, 3, 4); Proverbs 1–9 and throughout Jewish wisdom literature. On treating and curing people, compare a text of ritual power, Papyrus Oxyrhynchus 1384.15–22: "[Three men] met us in the desert [and said to the master] Jesus, 'What treatment is possible for the sick?' And he says to them, '[I have] given olive oil and have poured out myrrh [for those] who believe in the [name of the] father and the holy [spirit and the] son.'"

186. In general compare Unknown Sayings 4, 5, 6, 184, 187, 191.

187. Compare Unknown Sayings 143, 185, 186 (and parallels). On the gentle doctor, compare Unknown Sayings 15, 91, 132; Mark 2:17; Matthew 9:12; Luke 5:31; Papyrus Oxyrhynchus 1224, p. 175: "Those who are [well do not need a doctor]."

188. On the fallen rock, compare Gospel of Thomas sayings 102 (as well as one of Aesop's fables), 39 (see Unknown Saying 21). On drainpipes and graves, compare Matthew 23:27–28 (Q); Luke 11:44 (Q).

189. In general compare Unknown Sayings 7, 192, 193; Matthew 5:37; James 1:26; 3:1–12.

190. Contrast Unknown Saying 196.

191. On wisdom, in general, see the note to Unknown Saying 185.

192. Compare al-Ghazali, *Revival of the Religious Sciences*, 3.87: "Jesus said, 'Devotion is of ten parts. Nine of them consist in silence, and one in solitude'" (Margoliouth, "Christ in Islam," p. 107).

193. On "Go in peace," compare the common Semitic greeting (see Unknown Saying 79). On pigs, compare Unknown Saying 123 (and parallels). On the tongue, compare Unknown Saying 189 (and parallels).

194. On dogs, compare Unknown Saying 123 (and parallels).

195. Compare Matthew 8:20 (Q); Luke 9:58 (Q); Gospel of Thomas saying 86; Plutarch, Life of Tiberius Gracchus, has a similar statement; also Ibn 'Abd Rabbihi: "The Messiah said to the followers, 'I am the one who has turned the world upside down, for I have neither a wife, who can die, nor a house, which can be destroyed'" (based on the Latin in Asin, *Logia et Agrapha Domini Jesu*, p. 543).

196. On Jesus' homelessness, compare Unknown Saying 195 (and parallels); on his vegetarian diet, compare Unknown Say-

ing 32. On his wealth, contrast Unknown Saying 190. In contrast to Jesus' humble clothing, note the clothing described in al-Ghazali, *Revival of the Religious Sciences*, 3.269: "Jesus said, 'Luxury in clothing is pride of heart'" (Margoliouth, "Christ in Islam," p. 504). With this, compare Matthew 11:7–8 (Q); Luke 7:24–25 (Q); Gospel of Thomas saying 78: "Jesus said, 'Why have you come out to the countryside? To see a reed shaken by the wind? And to see a person dressed in soft clothes, [like your] rulers and your powerful ones? They are dressed in soft clothes, and they cannot understand truth.'" In general, compare a similar saying of Jesus from Ibn 'Abd Rabbihi: "Jesus said to the followers, 'Make the places of worship as houses and the houses as stopping places, and eat wild vegetables and drink pure water, and escape safe from the world'" (Muhammad 'Ata ur-Rahim, *Jesus, Prophet of Islam*, p. 224).

197. On seeking, compare Unknown Saying 3 (and parallels). In general compare also Unknown Sayings 196, 200 (and parallels).

198. On Jesus walking on water, compare Mark 6:45–52; Matthew 14:22–33; John 6:16–21 (in Matthew, Peter also tries to walk on water, but he sinks). In Greek mythology Poseidon is described driving his chariot over the water. On Jesus disregarding money, compare Unknown Saying 73; Matthew 10:7–16 (Q); Luke 10:2–12 (Q); also Matthew 6:24 (Q); Luke 16:13 (Q); Gospel of Thomas saying 47 ("A servant cannot serve two masters," to which Q adds, "You cannot serve God and wealth"). This saying in Q and Thomas in turn recalls another saying of Jesus from an Islamic source: "This world in relation to the future life is like a man who has two wives: if he pleases one, he will displease the other" (from the Latin in Asin, *Logia et Agrapha Domini Jesu*, p. 569).

199. Compare a Cynic *chreia*, or useful statement, cited by the Vatican grammarian, On the Chreia 24–28: "When Diogenes

the Cynic philosopher saw a country boy scooping up water in his hand in order to drink, he threw away the cup that he was carrying in his pack and said, 'Now I can be this much lighter'" (Greek text in Ronald F. Hock and Edward N. O'Neil, *The Chreia in Ancient Rhetoric*, 1.290–91).

200. The medieval author Petrus Alfonsi has a nearly identical saying (preserved in Latin) in his Clerical Instruction: "The world is like a bridge. Therefore, pass over it, only do not lodge there." Compare Gospel of Thomas saying 42; Unknown Saying 58; Jacut, *Geographical Lexicon*, 1.1: "Jesus said, 'The world is a place of transition, full of examples. Be pilgrims in it, and take warning by the traces left by those who have gone before'"; also Baidawi, *Commentary on the Qur'an*, p. 71: "Jesus said, 'Be in the midst, but walk on one side'" (Margoliouth, "Christ in Islam," p. 59). For additional parallels and discussion, see Jeremias, *Unknown Sayings of Jesus*, pp. 111–18.

Selected Bibliography

Asin y Palacios, Michael. *Logia et Agrapha Domini Jesu apud Moslemicos Scriptores.* In R. Graffin and F. Nau (eds.), *Patrologia Orientalis.* Paris: Firmin-Didot 13.3 (1919), 335–431; 19.4 (1926), 531–624; Turnhout, Belgium: Brepols, 1974.

Attridge, Harold W., ed. *Nag Hammadi Codex I (The Jung Codex).* 2 vols. Nag Hammadi Studies 22–23. Leiden: E. J. Brill, 1985.

Bauer, Walter. *Das Leben Jesu im Zeitalter der neutestamentlichen Apokryphen.* Tübingen: J. C. B. Mohr (Paul Siebeck), 1909; Darmstadt: Wissenschaftliche Buchgesellschaft, 1967.

Borg, Marcus, ed. *The Lost Gospel Q: The Original Sayings of Jesus.* Berkeley: Ulysses, 1996.

Bultmann, Rudolf. *History of the Synoptic Tradition.* Trans. by John Marsh. New York: Harper & Row, 1963.

Cameron, Ron. *Sayings Traditions in the Apocryphon of James.* Harvard Theological Studies 34. Philadelphia: Fortress Press, 1984.

Casey, R. P., and R. W. Thomson. "A Dialogue Between Christ and the Devil." *Journal of Theological Studies* 6 (1955): 49–65.

Crossan, John Dominic. *The Historical Jesus: The Life of a Mediterranean Jewish Peasant.* San Francisco: HarperSanFrancisco, 1991.

Duling, Dennis C., and Norman Perrin. *The New Testament: Proclamation and Parenesis, Myth and History*. Orlando: Harcourt Brace, 1994.

Dunkerley, Roderic. *Beyond the Gospels*. Middlesex: Penguin, 1957.

———. "The Muhammadan Agrapha." *The Expository Times* 39 (1927–28): 167–71, 230–34.

Emmel, Stephen, ed. *Nag Hammadi Codex III, 5: The Dialogue of the Savior*. Nag Hammadi Studies 26. Leiden: E.J. Brill, 1984.

Epstein, Isidore, ed. *The Babylonian Talmud*. 34 vols. London: Soncino, 1935–52.

Funk, Robert W. "Criteria for Determining the Authentic Sayings of Jesus." *The Fourth R* 3 (1990): 8–10.

———. *Honest to Jesus: Jesus for a New Millennium*. San Francisco: HarperSanFrancisco, 1996.

Hedrick, Charles W., and Paul A. Mirecki. *Gospel of the Savior: A New Ancient Gospel*. California Classical Library. Santa Rosa, Calif.: Polebridge, 1999.

Herford, R. Travers. *Christianity in Talmud and Midrash*. Clifton, N.J.: Reference Book Publishers, 1966.

Hock, Ronald F., and Edward N. O'Neil. *The Chreia in Ancient Rhetoric, Vol. 1: Progymnasmata*. Society of Biblical Literature Texts and Translations 27, Graeco-Roman Religion 9. Atlanta: Scholars, 1985.

Hofius, Otfried. "Agrapha." In Gerhard Krause and Gerhard Müller (eds.), *Theologische Realenzyklopädie*, vol. 2. Berlin/New York: Walter de Gruyter, 1978.

———. "Isolated Sayings of the Lord." In Wilhelm Schneemelcher (ed.), *New Testament Apocrypha*, vol. 1. Eng. trans. ed. by R. McL. Wilson. Cambridge: James Clarke; Louisville: Westminster/John Knox, 1991.

James, Montague Rhodes. *The Apocryphal New Testament*. Oxford: Clarendon, 1924, 1953.

Jeremias, Joachim. *Unknown Sayings of Jesus*. Trans. by Reginald H. Fuller. London: SPCK, 1957. 2nd ed., 1964.

Khalidi, Tarif, ed. *The Muslim Jesus: Sayings and Stories in Islamic Literature*. Cambridge, Mass., and London: Harvard University Press, 2001.

Klausner, Joseph. *Jesus of Nazareth: His Life, Times, and Teaching*. Trans. by Herbert Danby. New York: Macmillan, 1925; New York: Menorah, 1979.

Klimkeit, Hans-Joachim. *Gnosis on the Silk Road: Gnostic Texts from Central Asia*. San Francisco: HarperSanFrancisco, 1993.

Kloppenborg, John S. *Q Parallels: Synopsis, Critical Notes, and Concordance*. Foundations and Facets. Santa Rosa, Calif.: Polebridge, 1988.

——, Marvin W. Meyer, Stephen J. Patterson, and Michael G. Steinhauser. *Q-Thomas Reader*. Santa Rosa, Calif.: Polebridge, 1990.

Layton, Bentley, ed. *Nag Hammadi Codex II,2–7, Together with XIII,2*, Brit. Lib. Or. 4926(1), and P. Oxy. 1, 654, 655*. 2 vols. Nag Hammadi Studies 20–21. Leiden: E. J. Brill, 1989.

Mack, Burton L. *The Lost Gospel: The Book of Q and Christian Origins*. San Francisco: HarperSanFrancisco, 1993.

Margoliouth, D. S. "Christ in Islam: Sayings Attributed to Christ by Mohammedan Writers." *The Expository Times* 5 (1893–94): 59, 107, 177–78, 503–4, 561.

Mayotte, Ricky Alan. *The Complete Jesus*. South Royalton, Vt.: Steerforth, 1997.

Meyer, Marvin. *The Gnostic Gospels of Jesus*. San Francisco: HarperSanFrancisco, 2005.

——. *The Gospel of Thomas: The Hidden Sayings of Jesus*. San Francisco: HarperSanFrancisco, 1992.

——. *The Secret Teachings of Jesus: Four Gnostic Gospels.* New York: Random House, 1984.

Miller, Robert J., ed. *The Complete Gospels: Annotated Scholars Version.* Santa Rosa, Calif.: Polebridge, 1994.

Morrice, William G. *Hidden Sayings of Jesus: Words Attributed to Jesus Outside the Four Gospels.* Peabody, Mass.: Hendrickson, 1997.

Neusner, Jacob. *Aphrahat and Judaism: The Christian-Jewish Argument in Fourth-Century Iran.* Studia Post-Biblica 19. Leiden: E. J. Brill, 1971.

Parrinder, Geoffrey. *Jesus in the Qur'an.* New York: Oxford University Press, 1977.

Pick, Bernard. *Paralipomena: Remains of the Gospels and Sayings of Christ.* Chicago: Open Court, 1908.

Pines, Shlomo. *The Jewish Christians of the Early Centuries of Christianity According to a New Source.* Proceedings of the Israel Academy of Sciences and Humanities 2, no. 13. Jerusalem: Israel Academy of Sciences and Humanities, 1966.

ur-Rahim, Muhammad 'Ata. *Jesus, Prophet of Islam.* Elmhurst, N.Y.: Tahrike Tarsile Qur'an, 1991.

Resch, Alfred, ed. *Agrapha: Aussercanonische Schriftfragmente.* 1st ed., Texte und Untersuchungen zur Geschichte der altchristlichen Literatur 5,4 (1889). 2nd ed., Texte und Untersuchungen zur Geschichte der altchristlichen Literatur 15,3-4 (1906). Leipzig: J. C. Hinrichs; Darmstadt: Wissenschaftliche Buchgesellschaft, 1967.

Robbins, Vernon K. *Ancient Quotes and Anecdotes: From Crib to Crypt.* Santa Rosa, Calif.: Polebridge, 1989.

Robinson, James M., Paul Hoffmann, and John S. Kloppenborg, eds. *The Critical Editon of Q.* Minneapolis: Fortress; Leuven: Peeters, 2000.